The Revision
of Psychoanalysis

Interventions • Theory and Contemporary Politics
Stephen Eric Bronner, Series Editor

The Revision of Psychoanalysis, Erich Fromm

*Corporate Society: Class, Property, and
Contemporary Capitalism,* John McDermott

Television and the Crisis of Democracy, Douglas Kellner

FORTHCOMING

Congress and Class Struggle, John C. Berg

*Crises and Transitions: A Critique of the
New International Economic Order,* David F. Ruccio,
Stephen Resnick, and Richard D. Wolff

Social Regulation and the State, Charles Noble

The Revision of Psychoanalysis

Erich Fromm

edited by
Rainer Funk

Westview Press
Boulder • San Francisco • Oxford

Interventions: Theory and Contemporary Politics

Copyright © 1992 by the Estate of Erich Fromm

Published in 1992 in the United States of America by Westview Press, Inc., 5500 Central Avenue, Boulder, Colorado 80301-2847, and in the United Kingdom by Westview Press, 36 Lonsdale Road, Summertown, Oxford OX2 7EW

Library of Congress Cataloging-in-Publication Data
Fromm, Erich, 1900–
   [Entdeckung des gesellschaftlichen Unbewussten. English]
   The revision of psychoanalysis / Erich Fromm ; edited by Rainer Funk.
      p.   cm. — (Interventions—theory and contemporary politics)
   Includes bibliographical references and indexes.
   ISBN 0-8133-1451-8
   1. Psychoanalysis.   2. Subconsciousness—Social aspects.
3. Social psychology.   4. Sexual deviation.   I. Funk, Rainer.
II. Title.   III. Series.
BG173.F866413   1992
150.19′57—dc20   92-18300
                                                                 CIP

Printed and bound in the United States of America

10   9   8   7   6   5   4   3   2   1

First of all, man is a social animal.

Specifically, revised psychoanalysis will examine the psychological phenomena that constitute the pathology of contemporary society: alienation, anxiety, loneliness, the fear of feeling deeply, lack of activeness, lack of joy. These symptoms have taken over the central role held by sexual repression in Freud's time.

Psychoanalytic theory must be formulated in such a way that it can understand the unconscious aspects of these symptoms and the pathogenic conditions in society and family that produce them. In particular, psychoanalysis must study the "pathology of normalcy"—the chronic, low-grade schizophrenia that is generated by the cybernated, technological society of today and tomorrow.

These drives can be regressive, archaic, and self-destructive, or they can serve man's full unfolding and establish unity with the world under the conditions of freedom and integrity. In this optimal case, man's trans-survival needs are born not out of unpleasure and "scarcity" but out of his wealth of potentialities, which strive passionately to pour themselves into the objects to which they correspond: He wants to love because he has a heart; he wants to think because he has a brain; he wants to touch because he has a skin.

Contents

Contents

Foreword

In 1965 Erich Fromm became professor emeritus of psychoanalysis at the National Autonomous University of Mexico City. In the same year he finished his field research on the social character of the Mexican peasant village Chiconcuac. Released from his obligations at the university and free for a new project, he applied to various funding organizations for money to undertake a "Systematic Work on Humanistic Psychoanalysis," which he had decided to write in the course of the next few years. It was conceived as a work of three to four volumes that would deal with the complete range of psychoanalytic theory and practice. He intended nothing less than a dialectic revision.

Originally, Fromm wanted to write this "systematic and comprehensive work of psychoanalysis" against the backdrop of his clinical experience as a practicing psychoanalyst, teacher, and supervisor. He also wanted to enrich his project with a number of case histories. That was not to be. Although Fromm worked for years on the project, his interest over time increasingly shifted toward the problem of forming an adequate psychoanalytic theory of aggression. This work Fromm presented in 1973 in his comprehensive volume *The Anatomy of Human Destructiveness.*

Other aspects of his project remained unfinished or were realized only in terms of the theoretical aspects. Fromm published only one chapter out of this work: "The Crisis of Psychoanalysis" (Fromm, 1970c). It showed in detail the great need for the revision of psychoanalysis, even in its forms of further development as exemplified by the so-called Ego Psychologists. Fromm did not, however, publish his own position—his reformulation and re-vision of psychoanalysis.

This volume contains the until now unpublished parts of Fromm's humanistic and dialectic revision of psychoanalysis, conceived between 1968 and 1970. The largest cohesive manuscript part (Chapter 2) is therefore logically entitled "The Dialectic Revision of Psychoanalysis." Here Fromm develops his method of the "Psychoanalysis of Theories," which he used to revise Freud's theories. Fromm devoted special attention to the importance of social repression for a new definition of the unconscious. This chapter also contains important explanations of Fromm's perspective on therapeutic practice. And Fromm speaks for the first time here about his concept of transtherapeutic psychoanalysis, which in 1975 he included in *From Having to Being* (Fromm, 1989a).

Every revision of psychoanalysis must deal with the significance of sexuality to psychic processes. Fromm's critique of the role imputed to sexuality is expressed in the chapter entitled "Sexuality and Sexual Perversions." In Fromm's view the basic connection between primitive drives and sexuality is of no significance. He uses examples of pregenital sexuality, perversions, and, here especially, the sadistic perversion. This new formulation of the psychoanalytic doctrine on perversions led him to repeat his critique of Herbert Marcuse's theories. Presented in a separate chapter that Fromm originally wanted to publish as an "Epilogue" to his collection entitled *The Crisis of Psychoanalysis* (1970a), this chapter carried the title "Infantilization and Despair Masquerading as Radicalism." The literary debate with his former colleague, Marcuse, had already begun in 1955 (Fromm, 1955b, 1956b) and was continued in a critical chapter in *The Crisis of Psychoanalysis* (1970c, pp. 9–41). One clearly feels the immediacy and emotional character of this argument in the chapter that appears here for the first time: "The Alleged Radicalism of Herbert Marcuse."

In one of his proposals to seek funding for his planned multivolume work on psychoanalysis, Fromm described the origin of the cognitive processes that guided his interest in the scholarly reception of Freudian psychoanalysis:

> My knowledge of and interest in the fields of sociology led me at first to the application of psychoanalytic theory to social and cultural problems. My papers in this area, containing already the nuclear ideas of my later work, were published in 1932–34. These papers showed for the first time the applicability of psychoanalytic theory to social-cultural problems. . . . In the course of these studies I began to become critical of strictly Freudian theory, and tried to modify it. Briefly, I tried to preserve Freud's fundamental discoveries, but replacing his mechanistic-materialistic philosophy by a humanistic one. Not man as a machine, regulated by the chemically produced tension–de-tension mechanism, but man as a totality, in need of relating himself to the world, was the basis of my theoretical thinking.

What Fromm insinuates here in rather simple words signals his replacement of the Freudian concept of man and its related theory of drives with a fundamentally different metapsychology: Man is to be understood primarily as a social being; the unconscious is mainly of interest in terms of the social unconscious and social repression; and the fact that man is driven is not due to instinctual drives but to his dichotomical situation as man, which is manifest in specifically human needs. Moreover, the ways of satisfaction are always social processes. The conflict between the individual and society, inherent in the Freudian concept of man, is understood by Fromm as a historically conditioned antagonism between the productive and nonproductive character orientations of the individual as a social being.

Corresponding to this new approach, which Fromm sketches in the first chapter of the present volume, was his understanding of psychoanalysis as an analytical social psychology. For him the discovery of the social unconscious should be located in the therapeutic applications of psychoanalysis: Common sense, the constraints of circumstances and of so-called normalcy, and the self-evident are rationalized expressions of the fixation on idols and the belief in illusions and ideologies. All such rationalizations are, in reality, merely expressions of the "Pathology of Normalcy."

Because the original English manuscript of this book was not put together in the organized form you see before you, I made additional divisions in the text and created subtitles. Necessary editorial additions and omissions within the text are marked with brackets.

Rainer Funk
Tübingen, March 1992

1

On My Psychoanalytic Approach

There is a widespread assumption—not only in the scientific literature dealing with psychoanalysis and social psychology but also among the general public—that a basic contradiction exists between the biological and social (or cultural) orientations in psychoanalysis. Often the Freudian orientation is called biological and the theories of the so-called neo-Freudian schools (particularly those of H. S. Sullivan, K. Horney, and this writer) are called culturalist, as if they were opposed to a biological orientation. This juxtaposition between biological and cultural emphasis is not only superficial but plainly erroneous, at least as far as my own work is concerned. I do not discuss here Sullivan's or Horney's positions, in view of the fact that my own theoretical concepts differ on fundamental points from those of Sullivan and Horney, just as these two authors differ between themselves.

The idea that my points of view are anti- (or non-) biological is based on two factors: first, on my emphasis on the significance of social factors in the formation of character; and, second, on my critical attitude toward Freud's theory of instincts and the libido theory. Although it is true that the libido theory is a biological one, like every theory that revolves around the life process of the human organism, my critique of the libido theory concerns not its biological orientation as such but, rather, its very *specific* biological orientation—namely, that of a *mechanistic physiologism*, in which Freud's libido theory is rooted. I have criticized the libido theory and not Freud's general biological orientation. On the contrary, another aspect of Freud's biological orientation, his emphasis on the constitutional factors in the personality, I have not only accepted theoretically but have also considered in my clinical work. In fact, I have probably taken it a good deal more seriously than do most orthodox analysts, who often pay lip service to constitutional factors but, for all practical purposes, believe that everything in a patient is conditioned by his early experiences within the family constellation.

Freud arrived almost unavoidably at his particular mechanistic physiological theory. Considering the scarcity of hormonological and neurophysiological data at the time of Freud's original formulations, it was hardly avoidable that he should construct a model based on the concept of chemically produced inner tensions that become painful and on the concept of the release of accumulated sexual tension, a release that Freud labeled "pleasure." The assumption of the pathogenic role of sexual repression seemed all the more evident because his clinical observations were made among people belonging to the middle class, with its strong Victorian emphasis on sexual repression. The dominant influence of the concepts of thermodynamics may also have influenced Freud's thinking, as E. Ericson has remarked.

Recognizing that, in neuroses, facets other than those *usually* called sexual desire play a most important role, Freud extended the concept of sexuality to that of "pregenital sexuality" and thus assumed that his libido theory could explain the origin of the energy that moves all passionate behavior, including aggressive and sadistic impulses. Since the 1920s, quite in contrast to the physiological-mechanistic orientation of his libido theory, Freud developed a much wider biological approach in his conceptualization of the life and death instinct. In considering the life process as a whole, he assumed that the two tendencies—that toward life (i.e., toward the increased unification and integration called Eros) and that toward death and disintegration (called the death instinct)—are inherent in every cell of the living organism. The correctness of this assumption may be questionable, but the new concept, though highly speculative, offered a global biological theory concerning the passions of man.

From a biological standpoint it should be noted that Freud's earlier theory, in spite of its narrowness, was based on the assumption that it is in the nature of the living organism to want to live, whereas in his more profound biological theory of the second phase, he discarded the earlier notion and made the assumption that the aim of disintegration is as much a part of man's nature as that following life and survival. In place of the hydraulic model of increasing tension and the necessity to reduce it, then, the nature of living substance, with its inherent polarity of life and death, became the new basis for Freud's thought. But it is tragic that Freud, for many reasons, never clarified the basic contradiction between the earlier and later theories; nor did he even connect the two in a new synthesis.

As a parallel to the connection between necrophilia and anal sadism, I have tried to draw a connection between an element of Freud's libido theory and his concept of the death instinct. Freud, still clinging to his older concept that the libido is masculine, avoided the almost obvious step to connect Eros with male-female polarity, but restricted the concept of Eros to the general principle of integration and unification.

Although Freud's biological orientation is beyond doubt, it would be a distortion of his work to characterize it as biologically versus socially oriented. Quite in contrast to such a false dichotomy, Freud was always socially oriented as well. He never regarded man as an isolated being, separate from the social context; as he put it in *Group Psychology and the Analysis of the Ego:*

> It is true that individual psychology is concerned with the individual man and explores the paths by which he seeks to find satisfaction for his instinctual impulses; but only rarely and under certain exceptional conditions is individual psychology in a position to disregard the relation of this individual to others. In the individual's mental life someone else is invariably involved, as a model, as an object, as a helper, as an opponent; and so from the very first individual psychology, in this extended but entirely justifiable sense of the words, is at the same time social psychology as well. (Freud 1921c, p. 69)

It is true that when Freud thought of the social factor, he was mostly concerned with the family rather than with society as a whole or with classes within society; but this does not alter the fact that in his attempt to understand the development of a person he had to comprehend, first, the impact of social influences (the family) on the given biological structure.

The false dichotomy between biological versus social orientation also underlies the false dichotomy in which my work is classified—as "culturally" rather than "biologically" oriented. My approach has always been a sociobiological one. In this respect it is not fundamentally different from Freud's, but it sharply contrasts with that type of behavioristic thinking in psychology and anthropology which assumes that man is born as a blank sheet of paper on which culture writes its text, through the mediation of the all-pervasive influence of customs and education (i.e., learning and conditioning).

In the following pages I want to give a brief summary of the main points that express the sociobiological orientation (cf. Fromm 1932a, 1941a, and 1955a).

1. This orientation is based above all on the concept of evolution. Evolutionary thinking is historical thinking. We call historical thinking "evolutionary" when we deal with bodily changes that have occurred in the history of the development of animals. And we speak of historical changes when we refer to those that are no longer based on changes in the organism. Man emerged at a certain point in animal evolution, and this point is characterized by the almost complete disappearance of instinctive determination and by an increase in brain development that permitted self-awareness, imagination, planning, and doubt. When these two factions reached a certain threshold, man was born, and all his impulses from then on were motivated by his need to survive under the conditions that had arisen by this point in his evolution.

The "evolutionary" changes in living beings occur through changes in the physical structure, from the one-celled organisms to the mammals. The "historical" changes (i.e., the evolution of man) are not changes in man's anatomical or physiological structure but, rather, are mental changes, which are adapted to the social system into which he is born. The social system itself depends on many factors such as climate, natural resources, population density, means of communication with other groups, mode of production, and so on. The historical changes in man occur in the areas of intellectual capacity and emotional maturity.

An important remark must be added. Even though man has retained the anatomical and physiological constitution that was present when he emerged as man, knowledge of the behavior and neurophysiological processes of animals, especially mammals, is of considerable interest for the study of man. It goes

5

without saying that superficial analogies of the kind K. Lorenz is fond of making are of little scientific value, and that one has to be very careful about drawing any conclusion from animal and human behavior, precisely because man constitutes a system of his own characterized by the combination of weak instincts and a highly developed brain. But if one is aware of these pitfalls, the results of studies of animal behavior and of the neurophysiological processes in animals can be very stimulating for the study of man. Needless to say, the psychoanalytic study of man must make use of the neurophysiological findings concerning man. It is true that psychoanalysis and neurophysiology are sciences that use entirely different methods and, by necessity, do not proceed by tackling the same problems at the same time. Hence each science has to follow the logic of its own method. The synthesis of psychoanalytic and neurophysiological data is to be expected one day. But even before this happens, each branch of the science of man should not only know about and respect the other but should also stimulate the other by presenting data and posing questions that contribute to the research in both fields.

2. The sociobiological orientation is centered around the problem of survival. Its fundamental question is: How can man, given his physiological and neurophysiological apparatus, as well as his existential dichotomies, survive physically and mentally? That man must survive physically needs no explanation; but that he must also survive mentally requires some comment.

First of all, man is a social animal. His physical constitution is such that he has to live in groups and therefore must be able to cooperate with others, at least for the purposes of work and defense. The condition for such cooperation is that he must be sane. And in order to remain sane—that is, to survive mentally (and, in an indirect sense, physically)—man must be related to others. He must have a frame of orientation that permits him to grasp reality and to maintain a relatively constant frame of reference in an otherwise chaotic reality. In turn, this frame of reference enables him to communicate with others. He must also have a frame of devotion, including values, that enables him to unify and channel his energy in specific directions, thereby transcending mere physical survival. The frame of orientation is partly a matter of cognition, acquired by learning the thought patterns of his society. But to a large extent it is a matter of character.

Character is the form in which human energy is channeled during the process of "socialization" (relatedness to others) and "assimilation" (mode of acquiring things). Character is, in fact, a substitute for absent instincts. If man, whose actions are not determined by instincts, had to decide before every action *how* to act, he would be unable to act efficiently; his decisions would take too long to make and would lack consistency. But by acting according to his character, he acts quasi-automatically and consistently; and the energy with which his character traits are charged guarantees effective, consistent action beyond what the force of learning can accomplish.

Freud's "character traits" are assumed to be rooted in the libido—specifically, in the libidinally cathexed erogenous zones. In the revision of the character concept that I attempted, character is seen as a biologically necessary phenomenon—necessary because it guarantees the mental and physical survival of man. The concepts of socialization and assimilation as two aspects of character orientation are also based on the biological consideration of man's twofold need to relate to others and to assimilate things. As those familiar with my previous writings know, I have wholly accepted Freud's clinical description of the various character syndromes. The difference lies precisely in the different biological approaches. One additional point needs to be mentioned, however. For Freud the energy with which the character

7

traits are charged is libidinal—that is, sexual (in the broad sense in which Freud used this term). But as I have used the term, *energy* is the desire of the living organism to survive, channeled into various paths that enable the individual to react adequately to this task. *Energy* in a general sense, rather than in the narrow sense of sexual energy, was first used by C. G. Jung, who did not, however, connect it with the sociobiological function of character.

The sociobiological function of character determines the formation not only of the individual character but also that of the "social character." The social character constitutes the "matrix" or "nucleus" of the character structure of most members of a group. This character structure develops as a result of the basic experiences and mode of life common to that group. The function of the social character, from a sociobiological standpoint, is to mold human energy in such specific ways that it can be used as a "raw material" for the purposes of the particular structure of a given society. It should be noted here that there is no society "in general" but only various structures of society—just as there is no psychic energy "in general" but only psychic energy channeled in various ways characteristic of a given character structure.

The development of the social character is necessary for the functioning of a given society, and the survival of society is a biological necessity for the survival of man. Of course, this is not to say that a given social character guarantees the stability of a given society. When the social structure is too contradictory of human needs, or if new technical or socioeconomical possibilities emerge at the same time, the previously repressed character elements will arise in the most advanced individuals and groups and help transform society into one more humanly satisfactory. Character, the cement of society during periods of socioeconomic stability, becomes dynamite in periods of drastic change.

To sum up: There is no "cultural" versus "biological" orientation, the former expressed by Freud, the latter by the "cultural school" of Fromm. Quite aside from the fact that I am not the founder of a school but, rather, a psychoanalyst who has attempted to further Freud's theory by making certain revisions, my orientation is a sociobiological one in which the development of personality is understood as the attempt of man, having emerged at a certain and definable point of evolution of animal life, to survive by dynamic adaptation to the social structure into which he is born. The false dichotomy between cultural and biological orientation is due partly to the general tendency to turn ideas into convenient clichés, rather than to understand them, and partly to the ideology of the bureaucratically organized international Psychoanalytical Society, some of whose members and sympathizers seem to need an easily grasped label to rationalize their dislike for the ideas of those analysts who believe that psychoanalysis and the bureaucratic spirit are incompatible.

2

The Dialectic Revision of Psychoanalysis

THE NECESSITY FOR THE
REVISION OF PSYCHOANALYSIS

Revision is a normal process within science. Paradoxically, a theory that remains the same for sixty years without being revised does not truly remain the same but becomes a system of sterile formulae. The question that matters, then, concerns not revision as such but *what* is revised and in what direction the revision leads. Does it continue in the direction of the original theory, even if it changes many single hypotheses within the theory? Or does it reverse the direction, even though it claims to continue the thought already indicated by the master?

In considering this problem of "revisionism" we stumble upon a serious difficulty. Who is to decide what the essence of the original theory was? Obviously a monumental work of genius carried on for more than forty years grows and changes and, in the process, shows contradiction. It is necessary to understand its nucleus—its essence, as it were—as differentiated from the sum total of all its theories and hypotheses. But, we must further ask, who is to decide what this essence is? The founder of the system? That would, indeed, be the most desirable and most convenient solution for those who come after the master. But in most cases, unfortunately, the founder is unable to decide. Even the greatest genius is a child of his time, and he is influenced by its prejudices and modes of thought. Often he is so absorbed by the struggle with old views or the formulation of new and original ones that he loses his perspective on what actually constitutes the essence of his system. He may consider some details necessary for proceeding to new positions as being more important than do those by whom his discoveries have been accepted and, hence, are not in need of the auxiliary constructions.

Who else is to decide what is essential in a system? The authorities? This word may seem strange when used in connection with scientific discoveries. But it is nevertheless quite appropriate. Science is often administered by institutions and bureaucrats who determine the expenditure of money, the appointment of researches, and so on, and who, in fact, have a controlling influence over the direction of scientific development. This is not always the case, of course. But it was undoubtedly very much the case in the psychoanalytic "movement." Without discussing why this was so, I believe that the psychoanalytic bureaucracy has tried to determine which theories and therapeutic practices deserved to be called "psychoanalysis"— and I do not think that this choice has been very successful from a scientific standpoint. This is not surprising. The scientific bureaucracies, like all others, soon acquire vested interests regarding power, position, prestige; and by controlling theory they are able to control people.

How, then, can one determine the essence of any great theoretical structure, be it Platonism, Spinozism, Marxism, or Freudianism, if neither its creator nor the official bureaucracy can tell what the essence of that theoretical structure is? The answer to this question cannot be very satisfactory because it leaves us without any hard-and-fast rule; yet, in my opinion, it is the only one that is useful.

Discovering the essence of a system is primarily a historical task. What does this task require? Whoever tries to undertake it must determine which new and creative thoughts in the system contradicted the views and ideas generally accepted at the time. He must then proceed to examine the general climate of thought and personal experience that existed during the period in which the system was created, from a social perspective as well as in the context of the master's life. He must also study how the master tried to express his new discoveries in terms of keeping in touch with the thought of his time, so that neither he nor his pupils feel completely isolated or "crazy." The task, then, is to understand how the formulations of the original system have been influenced by the attempt to find a compromise between the new and the extant; and eventually how, in the process of social change, the core of the system can be widened, translated, and revised. In a short formula the most crucial point could be expressed thus: The essence of the system is that which transcends traditional thought minus the traditional baggage in which this transcending thought is formulated.

Returning now to the system that Freud created, I believe the crucial discoveries were as follows:

1. Man is largely determined by drives that are essentially irrational—drives that conflict with his reason, his moral standards, and the standards of his society.

2. Most of these drives are not conscious to him. To himself he explains his behavior as being the outcome of reasonable motives (rationalization), all the while acting, feeling, and thinking according to the unconscious forces that motivate his behavior.

3. Any attempt to bring into his awareness the presence and operation of these unconscious drives meets with an energetic defense—namely, resistance—which can take many forms.

4. Aside from his constitutional equipment, man's development is largely determined by circumstances operating in his childhood.

5. Man's unconscious motivations can be recognized by inference from (i.e., interpretation of) his dreams, symptoms, and unintentional small acts.

6. Conflicts between man's conscious view of the world and himself, on the one hand, and these unconscious motivating forces, on the other—if their intensity transcends a certain threshold—can produce mental disturbance such as neurosis, neurotic character traits, or general, diffused listlessness, anxiousness, depressiveness, and so on.

7. If the unconscious forces become conscious, a most particular effect ensues: The symptom tends to disappear, an increase in energy occurs, and the person experiences greater freedom and joy.

All of these seven points among Freud's findings have a special relationship to the historical time in which he worked. He lived both at the peak and at the end of the period of rationalism and enlightenment. He was a rationalist, inasmuch as he believed that the power of reason is capable of solving the riddles of life (to the extent that they *are* solvable). But he transcended rationalism by recognizing that man is motivated by irrational forces to a degree that the rationalism of the eighteenth century did not foresee. This discovery of man's irrationality and of the unconscious character of the irrational forces within him constitutes the most radical discovery of

Freud, through which he transcended, and in a sense defeated, the optimistic rationalism current in the middle-class thought of his century. He dethroned conscious thought from its superior place, but he gave reason an even stronger foundation through his critique of conscious thought. By rationally explaining the irrational, he put reason on a new and very much more solid basis.

But Freud might have become an advocate of pessimism and despair had he not discovered a method to liberate man from the power of irrational forces—by making the unconscious conscious. This principle (Freud once expressed it with the words "Where there is id there shall be ego") turned Freud's insight into man's irrationality into an instrument for man's liberation. Thus Freud created not only a new dimension for truth but also a new dimension for freedom. Political freedom and freedom of trade and in the use of property would mean little if man could not free himself from the irrational and unconscious forces within him. The free man is the one who knows himself, but knows himself in a new way—by penetrating the deceptive cover of mere consciousness, and by grasping the hidden reality within himself.

Freud thus challenged the rationalistic-optimistic picture of man deeply ingrained in the thinking and feeling of his time; yet he adhered to the contemporary frame of reference in other respects—most of all, in his admiration for and application of the methods of mechanistic materialism, whose leading exponents constituted a group of German professors: H.L.F. Helmholtz, E. Du Bois–Reymond, and E. von Brücke. The latter, Freud's master and chief (as the head of the psychological laboratory at the University of Vienna), made a lasting impression on his student, who readily acknowledged his gratitude and admiration for the teacher. Although Freud shifted from physiology, neurology, and psychiatry (as the term was then used) to psychology, he carried with him the basic concepts and methods with which he had been imbued through Brücke's work. He was seeking the physiological substratum of psychic energy (libido). And, in his thinking within the new field of psychoanalysis, he kept alive the "neurologing" of Brücke's laboratory. Energy cathexis, bound and free energy, shifts of energy—these were among the basic categories of his new thought. When all is said, the fact becomes clear that Freud's historically crucial discoveries were these: (1) the presence of powerful irrational forces motivating man, (2) the unconscious nature of these forces, (3) their pathogenic consequences (under certain circumstances), and (4) the curing and liberating effect of making the unconscious conscious.

Freud's discoveries were attacked by those psychiatrists and psychologists who did not understand them. They were also attacked by former students and adherents who had understood them but became critical and, at the same time, desirous of shaking off the yoke of Freud's superior role and his sometimes rigid refusal to revise. A. Adler and C. G. Jung are the best known among these rebels. They suggested well-taken revisions, some of which were later incorporated by Freud. Much earlier than Freud, Adler recognized the importance of aggressive and destructive impulses. And Jung liberated psychic energy from its narrow conceptualization as sexual energy and translated it into the concept of psychic energy. He also had a richer concept of symbolism and mythology than Freud. In particular, he maintained that man was not only, or even mainly, influenced by personal factors in his life; rather, he believed that these personal factors, such as one's mother, represented universal phenomena and archetypes that exert powerful influences over the lives of everybody, regardless of the personality of the particular mother. In the context of these conditions and revisions, there could not have been any reason, or at least any need, for a schism. Even Freud's own rigidity and the personal ambitions of Adler and Jung do not offer a sufficient explanation. The real reason and necessity for the break was the fact that both Adler and Jung, albeit in different ways, did not share Freud's basic position. Adler, though gifted and shrewd, was not one to stand on the border of rationalism, looking into the abyss of irrationality. On the contrary, he belonged to a group that represented a new, relatively superficial optimism, characteristic of the new middle class in Germany and Austria before and after World War I. No paradoxical or tragic dimension characterized this group's thought. It was convinced that the world was getting better and better, and that even handicaps and damages would be turned into advantages.

The same naive optimism existed among the reformist Austrian and German Social Democrats, of whom Adler was one. But Jung stood in an entirely different historical position. He was basically a romantic and an antirationalist. He represented the romantic tradition whereby the irrational was not the emergence of reason to be understood in order to be overcome but, on the contrary, the fountainhead of wisdom, to be studied, understood, and incorporated, so as to enrich and deepen life. Freud was interested in the irrational and the unconscious because he wanted to liberate man from his power. Jung was interested because he wanted to help and cure man by bringing him into contact with his unconscious. Freud and Jung were like two men who, while walking in opposite directions, meet at the same spot for a moment, get into an animated conversation, and forget that when they resume their walk they will increase the distance between them.

The third group of dissenters is usually called "neo-Freudians," "culturalists," or "revisionists." The main representatives of this group are Sullivan, Horney, and this writer. Of course, there were others, too, who disagreed considerably with the ruling orthodox beliefs, such as F. Alexander and S. Radó. But as they remained within the Freudian organization, the label of "neo-Freudian" was never applied to them.

The views of "neo-Freudians" are by no means identical. What they do have in common is a greater emphasis on cultural and social data than was customary among the Freudians. But certainly this emphasis was Freud's elaboration of the basic social orientation, which saw man in a social context always and attributed to society a crucial role in the process of repression. Sullivan placed less stress on sexuality and more on the avoidance of anxiety and insecurity. Horney emphasized the role of anxiety, of fears, and of incompatible ego-ideals. She also suggested fundamental changes in Freud's psychology of women. And, finally, the present writer, who became increasingly doubtful of the libido theory, suggested one in which the needs rooted in man's condition of existence took the center. He emphasized the role of society, not as "culture" but as a specific society structured along the lines of its mode of production and its main productive forces, and stressed the significance of value and ethical problems for the understanding of man.

None of the fundamental theories of Freud was attacked (in the sense mentioned above), nor did any of these three psychoanalysts try to form a new school that was to supersede Freud. They left the Freudian organization essentially because of the intolerance of the bureaucracy toward dissenters, not because of any will to found new organizations as the home for new or anti-Freudian systems. In this decisive respect they are entirely different from Adler and Jung. This difference is expressed symbolically by the fact that Adler and Jung gave their systems new names (Individual Psychology and Analytic Psychology, respectively), whereas the neo-Freudians insisted on keeping the word *psychoanalysis*—though not without the protest of some Freudians who claimed that anyone who did not follow the rules of the organization had no right to call himself a psychoanalyst. (The absurdity to which this bureaucratic spirit can lead is shown by the fact that five sessions per week and the use of the couch were made into criteria that decided whether or not somebody underwent psychoanalysis.)

From a scientific standpoint, the main fault of the founders of these new schools, Adler and Jung, was to "bagatellize" and later give up completely the great discoveries of Freud, and then to replace them with their own often inferior brands.

The neo-Freudians, including myself, may also be criticized for sometimes not having paid proper attention to Freud, or even for having been unnecessarily critical. Although such criticism is understandable, (especially in light of the Freudians' hostility), it is not, on the whole, either excessive or unbalanced. In spite of great differences among the neo-Freudians, they focused on the need to understand unconscious processes and the aim to make the unconscious conscious. However, none of them tried to find such formulations as would have appeased the Freudian bureaucracy and perhaps led to a friendlier reception of "neo-Freudian" thought.

SUBJECT AND METHOD OF THE
REVISION OF PSYCHOANALYSIS

A creative renewal of psychoanalysis is possible only if it overcomes its positivistic conformism and becomes again a critical and challenging theory in the spirit of radical humanism. (Cf. Fromm 1970c, p. 29.) This revised psychoanalysis will continue to descend ever more deeply into the underworld of the unconscious; it will be critical of all social arrangements that warp and deform man; and it will be concerned with the processes that could lead to the adaptation of society to the needs of man, rather than with man's adaptation to society.

Specifically, it will examine the psychological phenomena that constitute the pathology of contemporary society: alienation, anxiety, loneliness, the fear of feeling deeply, lack of activeness, lack of joy. These symptoms have taken over the central role held by sexual repression in Freud's time, and psychoanalytic theory must be formulated in such a way that it can understand the unconscious aspects of these symptoms and the pathogenic conditions in society and family that produce them.

In particular, psychoanalysis must study the "pathology of normalcy"—the chronic, low-grade schizophrenia that is generated by the cybernated, technological society of today and tomorrow.

I see the dialectic revision of classic Freudian theory as occurring—or continuing—in six areas: the theory of the drives, the theory of the unconscious, the theory of society, the theory of sexuality, the theory of the body, and psychoanalytic therapy. All have certain elements in common. One is the shift of philosophical background from mechanistic materialism to either historical materialism and process thinking or phenomenology and existentialism. A second element is the different concept of knowledge when applied to knowing a person, by contrast to knowledge as used in the natural sciences. We are dealing here with the fundamental difference between the Hebrew and the Greek ideas of knowledge. In the Hebrew concept, "to know" (*jada*) was essentially the active experience of a person, a concrete and personal relationship rather than an abstraction. (Cf. Fromm 1966a) H. S. Sullivan, in his formulation of the "participant observer," came close to referring to this kind of knowledge. And R. D. Laing has made it the basis of his whole approach to the patient. "To know" in the Hebrew sense also means both penetrating sexual love and deep understanding.

In the Greek, especially in Aristotle's works, knowledge of an object is impersonal and objective, and this kind of knowledge has become the basis for the natural sciences. Although the therapist also thinks in these objective terms when he considers many aspects of his patient's problems, his main approach must be the "knowledge of active experience"; this is the scientific method appropriate for the understanding of persons.

A third element is the revised model of man. Instead of the isolated and only secondarily social *homme machine,* we have the model of a primarily social being, who *is* only in the sense of being related and whose passions and strivings are rooted in the conditions of his existence as a human being. A fourth element is the humanist orientation, which assumes the basic identity of the potential in all human beings as well as the unconditional acceptance of the other as being no other than myself. And a fifth element is the socially critical insight into the conflict between the interests of most societies in the continuity of their own system as opposed to the interest of man in the optimal unfolding of his potentialities. This insight implies refusal to accept ideologies at face value; rather, it urges consideration of the search for truth as a process for liberating oneself from illusions, false consciousness, and ideologies.

The six areas of the productive development in psychoanalysis by no means are, or should be, separate from each other. On the contrary, they belong together, and it is to be hoped that in a revised system of psychoanalysis they will be integrated. It is unfortunate that until now there has been too little overlap among these areas. Nevertheless, it is convenient to treat them separately here in an attempt to clarify further what is meant by the "dialectic revision of psychoanalytic theory."

The dialectic revision follows two approaches. One calls for a reexamination of Freud's data and theoretical conclusions in the light of further data, a new philosophical framework, and the social changes that have occurred in the last few decades.

The second approach is a critique of Freud, based on what might be called "literary psychoanalysis." Every creative thinker sees further than he is able to express or is aware of. In order to formulate theories he must often close off a certain area of knowledge, thus never becoming aware that other possibilities exist or have their own validity. Naturally, he will choose those elements of observations and thought for which he has most evidence and which best fit into his own frameworks of philosophy, politics, and religion. Unless he made such a selection, he would be too much torn between the several possibilities involved in looking at and explaining data ever to arrive at a systematic theory. How then do we come to the conclusion that he unconsciously thinks also of other possibilities—in fact, is *ahead of himself?* It is really no different from what happens in psychoanalysis: We infer the presence of unconscious ideas by peculiar omissions, slips, under- or overstatements, hesitancies, abrupt transitions, dreams, and so on. In the case of literary psychoanalysis we use the same method, except that we have no dreams available. By analyzing the exact way in which a writer expresses himself, the immanent contradictions he has not completely smoothed out, the brief mention of a theory that is never taken up again, the overinsistence on certain points, and the omission of what he could have hypothesized, we can conclude that the author must have been aware of certain other possibilities—but so slightly aware that only occasionally do they find a brief overt expression. (For the most part they are truly repressed.) The need for and validity of such literary psychoanalysis will, of course, be denied either by those who deny the validity of psychoanalysis in general or by those who believe that the work of the psychologist, sociologist, historian, and so forth, is purely a product of intellect, uninfluenced by personal factors.

In contrast to personal psychoanalysis, literary psychoanalysis is primarily concerned not with repressed emotions or desires but with the repressed thought and distortions in the author's thinking. It aims to explore the hidden thought and to explain the distortions. To be sure, psychological considerations play an important part in such analysis. In the most obvious case, the author's fears stop him from arriving at logical conclusions and make him misinterpret his own data, or emotional prejudices make it impossible for him to see certain flaws in his theory or to think of better theoretical explanations. (The most drastic example in Freud's case was his patriarchal bias.) What really matters, however, is not so much the uncovering of emotional motivations but the reconstruction of ideas that, for whatever reasons, did not enter into the manifest content of the author's thoughts (or did so only in an indirect or transitory manner).

Of course, the reasons for the repression of certain insights differ very much from author to author. As mentioned before, one frequent reason for repressing what is unpopular or even dangerous is fear; another is deeply rooted affective "complexes"; still another is intense narcissism, which inhibits proper self-critique. In Freud's case it can be assumed that neither fear nor narcissism played an important part. But there is another motive that may be quite significant: Freud's role as the leader of the "movement." His adherents were bound together by the common theory; and if Freud had made drastic changes in it, he might have satisfied his passion for truth, but he would also have created confusion in the ranks of his adherents and thus endangered the movement. I think it possible that the fear of doing the latter might have sometimes tempered his scientific passion.

It should be emphasized that literary psychoanalysis does not claim to decide whether a theory is right or wrong. It only brings to light, provided the evidence exists, what an author

23

may have thought behind and beyond what he thought he thought. In other words, literary psychoanalysis can help us, as Kant once said, "to understand the author better than he understood himself." But the validity of the inferred possibilities can be argued only on the grounds of their scientific merits.

ASPECTS OF A REVISED THEORY OF DRIVES

In my own work, especially since 1941, I have attempted to develop a revised theory of the drives and passions that motivate men's behavior in addition to those that serve his self-preservation.

I have assumed that these drives cannot be explained adequately as being an inner-chemical process of tension and detension but, rather, are to be understood on the basis of man's "nature." However, this concept of the "nature" or "essence" of man (i.e., of that by virtue of which man is man) differs from all those concepts which postulate that man's essence can be described in positive terms, as a substance, or as a fixed structure with certain unchangeable qualities such as good or bad, loving or hating, free or unfree, and so on. *The "essence" of man is a dichotomy* that exists only in the human being. It is an opposition between *being in nature* and being subject to all its laws, and simultaneously *transcending nature,* because man, and only he, is aware of himself and of his existence; in fact, he is the only instance in nature where life has become aware of itself.

At the basis of this insoluble existential dichotomy (existential in contrast to historically conditioned dichotomies that can be made to disappear, like the one between wealth and poverty) lies an *evolutionary, biologically given fact:* Man emerges from animal evolution at the point where determination by instincts has reached a minimum, while at the same time the development of that part of the brain that is the basis for thinking and imagination has developed far beyond the order of size that is found among the primates. On the one hand, this fact makes man more helpless than the animal; on the other, it gives him the possibility for a new, albeit entirely different, kind of strength. Man *qua* man has been thrown out of nature, yet he is subject to it; he is a freak of nature, as it were. This *biological* fact of man's inherent dichotomy demands solutions; that is to say, it demands human development. From a subjective standpoint, the awareness of having been torn away from his natural basis, and of being an isolated and unrelated fragment in a chaotic world, would lead to insanity (the insane person is one who has lost his place in a structured world, one that he shares with others and in which he can orient himself). Hence the energies of man have as their aims the transformation of the unbearable dichotomy into a bearable one and the creation of ever new and, as far as possible, better solutions of the opposition. All of man's passions and cravings, whether normal, neurotic, or psychotic, attempt to solve his immanent dichotomy; and because it is vital for man to find a solution, they are charged with the entire energy inherent in a person. Broadly speaking, they are "spiritual," survival-transcending ways of escaping the experience of nothingness and chaos by finding some frame of orientation and an object of devotion; they serve mental rather than physical survival. (I have long been seeking an adequate formulation to denote the concept of "spiritual" or "spirituality," but I have not found one that seems to me as useful as the following one used by S. Sontag (1969, p. 3): "Spirituality—plans, terminologies, ideas of deportment aimed at resolving the painful structural contradiction, inherent in the human situation, at the completion of human consciousness, at transcendence." How-

25

ever, I would put "passionate striving" before "plans, terminologies, ideas. . . .")

The nature or essence of man, then, as this theory conceives it, *consists in nothing but the opposition inherent in man's biological constitution*—an opposition that *produces* different solutions. The essence of man is not identical with any one of these solutions. To be sure, the number and quality of the solutions are not arbitrary and unlimited but, rather, are determined by the characteristics of the human organism and its environment. The data of history, child psychology, psychopathology—as well as, particularly, that of the history of art, religion, and myths—make it possible to formulate certain hypotheses about possible solutions. On the other hand, as mankind has thus far lived under the principle of scarcity and hence force and domination, the number of such solutions has by no means been exhausted. With the possibility of achieving a social life based on abundance and hence the disappearance of crippling domination, new solutions to the existential dichotomy are likely to develop. This theory of the essence of man is dialectical; and it is in contradiction to those theories that assume a substance or a fixed quality to be the essence of man. But it also stands in contrast to the concepts of existentialism; indeed, it constitutes a critique of existentialist thought. (The views presented here center on the problem of human existence and for this reason could be called "existentialist." But such a designation would be misleading inasmuch as they have little connection with existentialism as a philosophy. A more adequate option, if one needed a descriptive term, would be to designate them as rooted in radical humanism.)

If existence precedes essence, what is existence as far as man is concerned? The answer can only be that his existence is determined by the physiological and anatomical data that are characteristic for all men, since man's emergence from the animal kingdom; otherwise, "existence" is an abstract and empty concept. If, however, the biological dichotomy not only characterizes man's existence physically but results in psychic dichotomies that demand solutions, Sartre's statement that man is nothing else but what he makes of himself (Sartre 1957) is untenable. What man can make of himself and what he desires are the various possibilities that follow from his essence, which in turn is nothing but his existential-biological and psychic dichotomy. But existentialism does not define existence in this sense. It must remain caught in a voluntaristic position because of the abstract nature of its concept of existence.

This concept of the specifically human passions that I have sketched is dialectic, in that it calls for an understanding of psychic phenomena as the outcome of opposing forces. It recommends itself, in my opinion, because, (1) it avoids the unhistorical concept of a definite substance or quality as the essence of man; (2) it avoids the error of an abstract voluntarism whereby man is not characterized by anything other than his responsibility and freedom; (3) it puts the understanding of the nature of man on the empirical basis of his biological constitution *qua* man, explaining not only what he has in common with animals but also, dialectically, which opposite forces are released when he transcends animal existence; and (4) it helps to explain the passions and strivings that motivate men, both the most archaic men and the most enlightened.

Man's inherent dichotomy is the basis for his passionate strivings. Which of these is activated and becomes dominant in the character system of a society or an individual depends largely on the social structures, which, by their specific practice of life, teachings, rewards, and sanctions, have a selective function with regard to the various potential drives.

The concept of passions or drives that are specifically human, because they are engendered by man's existential dichotomy, does not imply the denial of the existence of drives that are rooted in man's physiology and are shared with all animals, such as the need to eat, to drink, to sleep, and, to some extent, in order to ensure the survival of the race, the sexual drive. These drives underlie the physiologically conditioned need for survival, and, in spite of a certain degree of malleability, are fixed.

The fundamental difference between the theoretical framework presented here and the classic theory is that Freud tried to understand all human passions as being rooted in physiological or biological needs, and he made ingenuous theoretical constructions in order to uphold this position. In the present framework, however, the most powerful human drives are not those aimed at physical survival (in the normal situation, where that survival is not threatened) but those through which man seeks a solution of his existential dichotomy—namely, a goal for his life that will channel his energies in one direction, transcend himself as a survival-seeking organism, and give meaning to his life. Much clinical and historical evidence shows that the pursuit and satisfaction of his biological needs alone leaves man dissatisfied and prone to serious disturbances.

These drives can be regressive, archaic, and self-destructive, or they can serve man's full unfolding and establish unity with the world under the conditions of freedom and integrity. In this optimal case, man's trans-survival needs are born not out of unpleasure and "scarcity" but out of his wealth of potentialities, which strive passionately to pour themselves into the objects to which they correspond: He wants to love because he has a heart; he wants to think because he has a brain; he wants to touch because he has a skin. Man is in need of the world because without it he cannot be. In the act of relatedness to the world, he becomes one with his "objects," and the objects cease to be objects (Fromm 1968h, p. 11). This active relatedness to the world is *being;* the act of conserving and feeding one's body, property, status, image, and so on, is *having* or *using.* The examination of these two forms of existing, their relationship to the concept of ego as the subject of *having* and *using* and to the concept of self as the subject of *being,* the categories of activity and passivity, of attraction to life and attraction to death—these are the central problems for the dialectic revision of psychoanalysis.

I have undertaken the revision of classic theory concerning pregenital sexuality in *Man for Himself* (Fromm 1947a, Chapter III), to which I must refer the reader. The central point of this revision is the thesis that the "oral" and the "anal" characters are not an outcome of anal and oral excitation; rather, they manifest a specific kind of relatedness to the world that is a response to the "psychic atmosphere" in the family and society.

Two passions seem especially to require a thorough revision: *aggression* and *Eros.* By not differentiating among qualitatively different classes of aggressiveness—for example, among reactive aggression in defense of vital interests, sadistic passion for omnipotence and absolute control, and necrophilous destructiveness directed against life itself—Freud and most other psychoanalytic authors blocked the way to understanding the genesis and dynamics of each of them. New theories of the various kinds of human aggressiveness are not only scientifically warranted but especially needed in a world gravely in danger of not being able to cope with the aggressiveness it engenders (Fromm 1973a).

In recent years a hypothesis, first presented in *The Heart of Man* (Fromm, 1964a), has been confirmed by many clinical observations made by myself and others (especially by M. Maccoby, 1976). I refer to the idea that the two most fundamental forces that motivate man are biophilia (the love of life) and necrophilia (the love of death, decay, and so on). The biophilous person is the person who loves life, who "brings to life" all that he touches, including himself. The necrophilous person, like Midas, transforms everything into something dead, unalive, mechanical. Nothing more than the relative strength of biophilia and necrophilia is what determines the whole character structure of a person or a group. This concept is a revision of Freud's life-and-death instinct based on clinical observation; but in contrast to Freud, the two tendencies are not biologically given forces present in every cell; rather, necrophilia is seen as a pathological development that occurs when, for a number of reasons, biophilia is blocked or destroyed. I believe that the further investigation of biophilia and necrophilia will be an important task for the dialectic revision of psychoanalysis.

The revision of Freud's concept of love is bound up with the examination of the concepts of libido and Eros. Freud did not view the male-female attraction as a *primary* phenomenon underlying sexual desire, because he saw sexual desire as produced by inner chemical processes and tensions that demand release. Aside from the attractiveness of this physiological explanation there is probably another reason Freud could not see male-female polarity as a primary phenomenon: Polarity implies equality (though also difference), and his strictly patriarchal viewpoint made it impossible for him to think in terms of male-female equality. Freud's concept of sexuality did not include Eros. He believed that the sexual drive was produced by an inner chemical process within the male, and that the female was the proper object for the drive.

When Freud developed his theory of Eros against the death instinct, he could have changed his position and suggested that Eros was the specific male-female attraction, in the sense of Plato's myth—that male and female were originally united and longed for a new union after separation had occurred. Ironically, this concept would have held the great theoretical advantage of permitting Freud to consider Eros as fulfilling his qualification for an instinct—namely, the tendency to return to an earlier condition. But Freud declined to move in this direction—again, I believe, because it would have implied accepting male-female equality.

Freud's theoretical difficulty regarding the problem of love and Eros was indeed considerable. Just as he had not considered aggression a primary drive in his earlier work (although he also never neglected it altogether), he believed love to be an epiphenomenon: "aim-inhibited" sexuality. Love's substrate was sexuality, conceived in the spirit of Freud's physiologizing frame of reference. Indeed, his original concept of sexuality and his later concept of Eros cannot be reconciled. They are based on entirely different premises: Eros, like the death instinct, is not localized in a specific erogenous zone; it is not regulated by inner, chemically produced tensions and the need for de-tension. Furthermore, unlike the libido it is not subject to evolution but, rather, is an essentially fixed quality of all living substance. Nor does it live up to Freud's requirements for an instinct: I have already referred to Freud's admission that Eros did not have the conservative nature he once assumed essential for an instinct. O. Fenichel (1953, pp. 364ff.) has made the same point with regard to Freud's concept of the death instinct.

Freud did not call attention, however, to the fundamental difference between the two concepts of drives, nor was he perhaps fully aware of it. He tried to fit the old and the new concepts together, so that the death instinct took the place of the former aggressive instinct and Eros took the place of sexuality. But one can recognize the difficulty he found in this endeavor. He speaks of "the sex instinct understood in the widest sense" and suggests that it can also be called Eros "if you prefer the name" (Freud 1933a, p. 103). In *The Ego and the Id* (1923b, p. 40), Freud identifies Eros with the sexual instinct and the instinct for self-preservation. In *Beyond the Pleasure Principle* (1920g, pp. 60ff.), he suggests that the sexual instinct was "transformed for us into Eros," which seeks to force together the portions of living substance. "What are commonly called the sexual instincts are looked upon by us as the part of Eros which is directed toward objects." And in his last work, *An Outline of Psychoanalysis* (1940a, p. 151), he states that the libido is an exponent of Eros (rather than, as earlier asserted, that Eros is the transformed libido), and that according to "our theory" they do *not* coincide.

I believe that a "literary psychoanalysis" of Freud's theories on sexuality and love would show that his own thinking was leading to a new appreciation of love, both as a primal force of life and in its specific form of male-female attraction. Underneath the theory as he expressed it was a concept in which love of life, love between man and woman, love of fellow humans, and love of nature were only different aspects of one and the same phenomenon. One may assume that these new concepts were not fully conscious to Freud and that they reveal their existence only in certain inconsistencies, surprising but isolated statements, and so forth. As an example of the inner wavering of Freud, the following may serve: In *Civilization and Its Discontent* he commented on the command "Love thy neighbor as thyself" with the words: "What is the point of a precept enunciated with so much solemnity if its fulfilment cannot be recommended as reasonable?" (Freud 1930a, p. 110). And in his letter to Einstein published in *Why War?* he wrote: "Anything that encourages the growth of emotional ties in men must operate against war. This is no reason for psychoanalysts to be ashamed to speak of love in this connection, for religion itself uses the same words 'thou shalt love thy neighbor as thyself'" (Freud 1933b, p. 212). Such a hypothesis, being a matter of interpretation and conjecture, cannot be "proven"; but much evidence can be adduced in its favor, thus suggesting the possibility that a deep conflict was going on in Freud's own thought. Inasmuch as this conflict never became fully conscious, he was simply forced to deny it and to declare that there was no contradiction between the concept of sex and the new theory of Eros. Whatever the merits of this interpretation, I believe that dialectic revision ought to study the contradictions between Freud's older and later theories, and to search for new solutions—some of which, indeed, Freud might have arrived at had he lived longer. (A detailed analysis of Freud's libido and Eros concept is to be found in the appendix to my book *The Anatomy of Human Destructiveness* [1973a].)

REVISION OF THE THEORY OF THE
UNCONSCIOUS AND THE REPRESSED

Unconsciousness and the Repression of Sexuality

Freud's central discovery was that of the unconscious, and of repression. He linked these key concepts with his libido theory and assumed that the unconscious was the seat of the instinctive sexual desires. (Later he would assert that parts of the ego and the super-ego were also unconscious.) Unfortunately, however, this connection facilitated a development that hobbled psychoanalytic thinking.

First, all interest was concentrated on sexual content, genital and pregenital, and the only interesting aspect of the unconscious was repressed sexuality. Whatever the merits of the libido theory, Freud created an instrument to know oneself that extended far beyond the sexual realm, into all areas of the unconscious. I, the person, am greedy, frightened, narcissistic, sadistic, masochistic, destructive, dishonest, and so on and on; but my awareness of all these qualities is repressed. If I concentrate all my interest on my repressed sexual and erotic strivings, I can live with this kind of analysis very comfortably, especially if I believe that sexuality—both genital and pregenital—is good and should neither be repressed nor suppressed. I do not have the painful task of seeing that side of myself which does not correspond to my conscious self-image.

Restricted to the libido, the great discovery of Freud loses much of its truly critical and unmasking character; it is apt to be used simply as a tool to analyze others (those who still have not liberated themselves from the sexual taboos) rather than as an instrument to know myself and to change myself. We cannot dismiss this type of psychoanalysis by calling it therapy and saying that it belongs in the office of the clinician. The therapy may have some technical character, but the phenomenon itself— the understanding of my own unconscious and its incompatibility with my conscious image of myself—is precisely the discovery that gives psychoanalysis its importance as a radical step in man's self-discovery and toward a new form of sincerity. But, unfortunately, it has become fashionable to apply the concept of repression exclusively to sex, and to believe that if there is no repression of sexual desires, the unconscious has been made conscious.

The lack of repression of sexual desires does not mean that most of the unconscious has been made conscious—a fact clearly demonstrated by those social groups in which sexuality in all its forms is freely practiced and experienced, without the burden of the traditional feelings of guilt. This is, indeed, one of the remarkable changes occurring in Western society today. Also remarkable is the fact that this free and "guiltless" experience of sex is to be found not only in the politically radical groups of the youth but also among the nonpolitical hippies and the politically unradical middle-class youth of North America and Western Europe. Furthermore, it exists in certain circles of the middle-aged in the affluent middle class. Apparently the sexual liberation for which W. Reich was the most gifted spokesman is occurring with amazing speed in all groups of the consumer society, but without the political consequences Reich assumed would follow.

The important problem is to understand the *quality* of sexual experience. In large measure, sexual gratification has become an article of consumption and now has the characteristics of all other modern consumption; motivated largely by boredom, hidden depression, and anxiety, the act of satisfaction itself is shallow and superficial.

It strikes me that much of the sexual motivation among those of the younger radical generation is somewhat prompted by theoretical considerations along the lines of Freud and Reich. Sexual satisfaction as a way of getting rid of all one's "complexes" can become somewhat obsessional, especially when it goes together with anxious self-examination about an "adequate" orgasm and so on. Group sex, though much can be said for it theoretically (such as that it overcomes jealousy or the sense of property), may in practice not be as different from the conventional bourgeois extramarital sex life (including voyeurism and exhibitionism) as its participants think. This holds true especially with respect to the need for new and different sexual partners because interest in the same partner has quickly waned.

Although the emancipation of sexual satisfaction from feelings of guilt is an important step forward, the question remains as to what extent the "radical" youth suffer from the same defect as their elders and their more conventional peers—namely, the inability to achieve human intimacy, a defect for which sexual and political intimacy is substituted. The next step for the youth of the radical generation, it seems to me, is to become more aware of their fear of deep emotional intimacy and the role of sex as a substitute. In addition, there seems to me to be a

tendency among the same people who so firmly reject dogma-
tism in their political thinking to follow half-digested psychoanalytic doctrines as a guide for their sex lives. To follow Freud,
even if fully digested, leads to an overemphasis on sex and to
the neglect of Eros and of love (as I shall try to show later in
this chapter). To mold one's sexual behavior according to Freud's
doctrines now seems somewhat old-fashioned and "radical"
only in terms of the older generation.

But sexual liberation does not mean that those participating
in the new freedom have lost most of their repressions, which
in any case are not so much less than those of their grandparents;
what has changed is the content of that which is repressed. By
looking for the unconscious mainly in the realm of sexuality,
we will have greater difficulty discovering other unconscious
experiences.

The deterioration of the concept of the unconscious is still
much more extensive when applied in an abstract sense, and
when it refers mainly to such general concepts as Eros or death
instinct. In this event, it loses all personal meaning and is in no
way an instrument for personal self-discovery.

Even the Oedipus complex (in Freud's scheme, the center of
repression) hardly touches the depth of unconscious human
passions. In fact, the boy's wish for sexual intercourse with the
mother, scandalous as it may seem from a conventional standpoint, is actually nothing irrational; the Oedipus complex is the
love triangle of adults retranslated into the infantile situation.
The child acts quite rationally—in fact, more so than adults
often do in similar situations. The little boy, prompted by his
budding sexuality, wants mother because she is the only, or the
most available, woman around; confronted with the rival-father's
castration threat, self-preservation wins over sexual passion;
then he gives up mother and identifies with the aggressor.

The Unconscious and the
Repression of Mother Fixation

Behind the boy's tie to the mother on the genital level exists a much deeper and more irrational tie. The infant—boy or girl—is tied to mother as the life-giving, all-helping, all-protecting, all-loving figure; mother *is* life, *is* security; she shields the child from the reality of the human situation, which requires activity, making decisions, taking risks, being alone, and dying. If the tie with mother could be kept intact throughout life, life would be bliss; and the dichotomy of human existence would not have to be faced. Thus the infant clings to mother and resists leaving her. (At the same time, his own physical maturation as well as general cultural influences constitute a counter-trend that eventually, in the case of normal development, makes the child give up mother and find love and intimacy in relationships in which he acts, ideally, as an independent person.) The deep longing to remain an infant is usually repressed (i.e., unconscious) because it is incompatible with the ideals of adulthood with which the child is imbued by a patriarchal society.

A complicated issue to be studied further is the question as to what degree the tie to mother is cut in matricentric societies. In such societies (some of which are still in existence), private property, hired labor, and development of individuality are minimal. (In a primitive society the initiation rites have the function of breaking this tie drastically.) However, in the form that I have just described, the refusal to accept the full burden of individuation has still not lost rationality and contact with reality. The person may find a mother figure or a representation to whom he can remain attached in reality, one who dominates (or serves) and protects him; he can, for instance, attach himself to a motherly woman, or to an institution such as a monastery. But the refusal to be separated from mother can take on more extreme forms: Deeper and still more irrational than the wish to be loved and protected by mother throughout life is the craving to be one with her, to return to her womb, and eventually to undo the fact of having been born; then the womb becomes the grave, the mother earth in which to be "buried," the ocean in which to drown. There is nothing "symbolic" in this. The cravings are not "disguises" for repressed Oedipus strivings; on the contrary, the incestuous strivings are often an attempt to save oneself from the deeper, life-threatening cravings for mother. The deeper and more intense these cravings, the more repressed they are. Only in the case of psychosis and in dreams do they become conscious.

Classic psychoanalysis has not taken account of the depth of these cravings. Nor has it given proper weight to the fact that the primary tie of the infant (boy or girl) is to the mother. It was not until 1931 that Freud, in *Female Sexuality,* made a significant revision of his earlier theory by stating that the "pre-Oedipus phase [pre-Oedipus attachment to mother preceding the attachment to father] in women gains an importance which we have not attributed to it hitherto" (Freud 1931b, p. 226). It is interesting that Freud compares this pre-Oedipal attachment to mother with matriarchal society: "Our insight into this early, pre-Oedipus phase in girls comes to us as a surprise, like the discovery, in another field, of the Minoan/Mycean civilization behind the civilization of Greece" (Freud 1931b, p. 226).

In *An Outline of Psychoanalysis* Freud takes still another step. He writes: "In these two relations [feeding and care of the child's body] lies the root of a mother's importance. *Unique, without parallel, established unalterably for a whole lifetime as the first and strongest love object and as a prototype of all later love relations—for both sexes.* In all this *the phylogenic foundation has so much the upper hand over personal accidental experience* that it makes no difference whether a child has really sucked at the breast or has been brought up at the bottle and never enjoyed the tenderness of a mother's care" (Freud 1940a, p. 188. Emphasis added.) It certainly seems that, at the end of his life, Freud was presenting a theory that drastically contradicted his previous position. After describing the depth of the pre-Oedipus tie to mother, he states that it exists both in girls and in boys (in *Female Sexuality* he discussed it only in terms of girls) and that it exists on phylogenetic grounds, regardless of the actual feeding and body-caring that has taken place. However, Freud does not introduce this statement as a radical revision; instead, it follows his traditional comments about how the mother establishes ties to the infant by feeding him and taking care of his body.

The almost casual manner in which Freud made this addition can be explained only by literary psychoanalysis. I assume that Freud had been occupied for years with the possibility that a number of older assumptions were not correct—for example, assumptions about the exclusively sexual meaning of the Oedipus complex, and the negation of a deep, life-lasting tie to mother in boys and girls. He could not, however, bring himself to make the changes explicit and to clarify which of the older elements of the theory had been dropped and which new concepts had replaced them. It is as if certain new ideas, such as the one we are dealing with here, had been unconscious and were now expressed in a "Freudian slip"; in writing this statement, Freud probably was not aware of the extent to which it contradicted his previous assumptions.

Most psychoanalysts, even after 1931, did not take Freud's hint seriously enough to revise their older theoretical thinking. In John Bowlby's study "The Nature of the Child's Tie to the Mother" (Bowlby 1958), one also finds a detailed history of psychoanalytic thinking in the problem of the child's tie to mother. Bowlby's interpretation of Freud's statement is similar to Freud's own, but with the qualification that it is one possible interpretation and that he would like to believe "that it is correct."

C. G. Jung, too, made a very important contribution by pointing to the universal nature of "mother" and asserting that the individual empirical mother gains her real meaning only if one sees her as an "archetype." He postulates a "collective unconscious" on the basis of myths, rituals, symbols, and so on, and is forced to assume an inherited mode of psychic functioning, taking very lightly the difficulty of assuming that acquired characteristics can be inherited. This difficulty is avoided if one starts out, as here, with the concept of the existential dichotomy, inherent in man *qua* man, which is the condition for the development for the various "primordial" solutions in man throughout all his history.

Classic psychoanalysis failed to see the depth and irrationality of the craving for mother, but also the fact that this craving is not merely an "infantile" striving. It is true, genetically speaking, that the infant for biological reasons passes through a phase of intense "mother fixation"; but this is not the "cause" of the later dependence on mother. This tie to mother can retain its force—or the individual can regress to this solution—precisely because it is one of the "spiritual" answers to human existence. True enough, it may lead to absolute dependence, insanity, or suicide—but it is also one of the possibilities open to man in his attempt to find a solution to the existential dichotomy. To explain the fixation to mother on a sexual basis, or as repetition-compulsion, is to miss the true character of this answer to existence.

All these considerations have led me to assume that the central issue is not really "attachment to mother" but what we might well call "paradisical existence," characterized by the attempt to avoid reaching full individuation and, instead, living in the fantasy of absolute protectedness, security, and at-homeness in the world, at the expense of individuality and freedom. This fantasy is a biologically conditioned state of normal development. But we would be thinking too much in genetic terms if we were to focus on the attachment to mother, rather than on the function of this experience. It is necessary to study much more closely its total structure—the role of narcissism, the fear of fully perceiving reality, the wish for "invulnerability" and omniscience, the proneness to depression, the sense of total aloneness when the experience of invulnerability is threatened, and many more elements.

The same principle can be demonstrated with regard to other drives that are usually unconscious. An example is the anal-hoarding striving. In its most rational forms this striving is a clinging to possession, interpreted by the classic theory as the sublimation of the wish to retain the feces. But behind this craving is a less purposeful one: that of finding an answer to existence by absolute possession, absolute control; by transforming everything that is alive into dead matter; and, eventually, by worshiping death. This is another answer to the human dilemma, which in its extreme forms becomes incompatible with the process of living; if one interprets it as the result of anal eroticism, one shuts the door to understanding the depth and intensity of this solution. The same holds true for sadism and masochism as well as for narcissism.

After all, it should be remembered, as one looks at man's existence as a whole, that the adult is not so different from the child in his helplessness toward the forces that determine his life. He is much more aware of them and of how little he can do to control them, and his helplessness is on an adult level. But, in a certain sense, this helplessness is not less than that of the child. Only the full unfolding of all his potentialities can enable him to face his objective helplessness while not seeking shelter in the "paradise phantasy."

The Fixation on Idols as an Expression of the Social Unconscious

From this helplessness of man an extremely important phenomenon follows: The average person, regardless of his early relationship to mother and father, carries within himself a deep longing to believe in an all-powerful, all-wise, and all-caring figure. But there is more than "belief" in this relationship. There also exists an intense affective bond to this "magic helper." It is often described as "awe" or "love"; but sometimes it is not given any particular name. It resembles the attachment of the child to mother and father, in being essentially passive, hoping, trusting. But this passivity by no means reduces the intensity of the bond; if anything, it increases that intensity; inasmuch as one's life (as in the case of the infant) seems to depend on not being abandoned. In many instances the intensity of this bond far surpasses that of the ties to persons close to one in ordinary life. Of course, the less satisfaction there is in these ties, the more intense is the bond to the "magic helper." Only through belief in the support of this figure can the person cope with his sense of helplessness. Such figures can be religious idols, natural forces, institutions and groups (such as the state or nation), charismatic or simply powerful leaders, or individuals such as father and mother, husband and wife. It also makes little difference whether these figures are real or only imaginary.

I suggest that we call all of these figures by the generic name "idols." An idol is the figure to which a person has transferred his own strength and powers. The more powerful the idol grows, the more impoverished the individual himself becomes. Only by being in touch with the idol can he try to be in touch with himself. The idol, the work of his hands and fantasy, stands over and above him; its maker becomes his prisoner. Idolatry, in the sense of the Old Testament prophets, is essentially the same concept as that of "alienation." (Cf. Fromm 1966a.)

42

Only "idology," the full study of all "idols," could give a satisfactory picture of the intensity of the passion to find an idol and of the variety of idols that have existed in history. At this point I want to mention only one specific typology of idols: the mother- and father-type idol. The mother idol, as described above, is the unconditionally loving figure, the attachment to whom, however, stands in the way of full individuation. And the father idol is the strict patriarch whose love and support depend on obedience to his commands.

What evidence is there for the hypothesis that the average man is in need of an "idol"? The evidence is so overwhelming that it is hard to select the data. First of all, the greater part of human history is characterized by the fact that the life of man has been permeated by religions. Most of the gods of these religions have had the function of giving man support and strength, and religious practice has consisted essentially in appeasing and satisfying the idols. (The prophetic and later Christian religions were originally anti-idolatric; in fact, God was conceived as the anti-idol. But in practice the Jewish and Christian God was experienced by most believers as an idol, as the great power whose help and support could be attained through prayer, ritual, and so forth.) Nevertheless, throughout the history of these religions a battle was fought against the idolization of God—philosophically, by the representatives of "negative theology" (e.g., Maimonides) and, experientially, by some of the great mystics (e.g., Meister Eckhart or Jacob Boehme).

But idolatry by no means disappeared or was weakened when religion lost its power. The nation, the class, the race, the state, the economy, became the new idols. Without the need for idols one could not possibly understand the emotional intensity of nationalism, racism, imperialism, or the "cult of personality" in its various forms. One could not understand, for instance, why millions of people were ecstatically attracted to an ugly demagogue like Hitler; why they were willing to forget the demands of their consciences and to suffer extreme hardship for his sake. People's eyes shine with religious fervor when they see, or can touch, a man who has risen to fame and who has, or might have, power. But the need for idols exists not only in the public sphere; if one scratches the surface, and often even without doing so, one finds that many people also have their "private" idols: their families (sometimes, as in Japan, organized as ancestor cults), a teacher, a boss, a film star, a football team, a physician, or any number of such figures. Whether the idol can be seen (even if only rarely) or is a product of fantasy, the one bound to it never feels alone, never feels that help is not near.

One important question must be raised here: Why is it that there are groups and individuals in whom the attachment to an idol is so striking that it cannot be doubted, whereas in others it seems to be absent or, as I would suggest, latent or unconscious?

There are a number of reasons why this is so. These reasons can, in principle, be found either in the external conditions of life or in the psychological structure of the person(s) involved, the latter being mostly the function of the former.

Among the external reasons the most important are poverty, misery, economic insecurity, and hopelessness. Among the subjective psychological reasons are anxiety, doubt, subclinical depression, a sense of impotence, and many neurotic and semineurotic phenomena. In such cases one often finds the presence of anxiety-producing or infantilizing parents.

In contrast to these two categories of people, in whom the need for an idol is permanent and manifest, are others in whom this need becomes manifest only if certain new conditions arise. Normally, when everything is going well, when people are satisfied with the conditions of their existence, their work, and their income, when they experience a sense of identity by fulfilling the role attributed to them by society, when they can hope to rise on the social ladder, and so on, their need for the idol remains latent. But when this equilibrium of relative satisfaction is disturbed by sudden traumatic circumstances, the latent need becomes manifest. On the social scale such traumatic events include, for example, severe economic crisis leading to mass unemployment, drastic inflation, intense insecurity (such as the crisis of 1929, which in Germany led to the rise of Hitler), and war. (The saying during World War I that "there are no atheists in the trenches" was very much to the point.) On the individual scale such events may include severe illness, socioeconomic failure, and the death of beloved persons.

However, such traumatic events are not the only causes that activate the latent need for an idol. Frequently, this latent desire is awakened when someone who fits the role of an idol enters into a person's private life and mobilizes the "idolatric passion." This can occur in various ways: The person might be particularly kind or wise or helpful and may thus provoke the longing for an idol; or he might be strict and threatening, treating the other as a child. The latter can indeed have the same traumatic effect, as would a combination of the two factors.

The Fixation on Idols and the Phenomenon of Transference

The most frequently observable example of the mobilization of the "idolatric passion" is the phenomenon of "transference." Freud discovered that patients regularly developed intense feelings of dependence on, awe of, or love for him during psychoanalytic treatment. Since then, every analyst has had the same experience. In fact, transference is one of the most obvious and yet puzzling phenomena known to psychoanalysis. Regardless of the actual characteristics of the analyst, many patients not only have an extremely idealized and unreal picture of him or her but also develop a deep attachment that is often very difficult to break. A friendly word can create a state of well-being and happiness; and the absence of a friendly smile, due to any number of causes having nothing to do with the patient, can cause deep feelings of unhappiness or anxiety. It often seems that no person in the life of the patient can influence his mood to the extent that the psychoanalyst can. That this tie is not caused by sexual desires is proven by the fact that it exists regardless of the respective sexes of analyst and patient. (However, in cases where the two are of different sexes, the "love" for the analyst can have strong sexual overtones, inasmuch as strong affective bonds often arouse sexual desires in persons of different sexes and of suitable ages.)

Although transference is a phenomenon that occurs regularly in the psychoanalytic treatment situation, its intensity varies greatly depending on a number of conditions. One such condition is severe neurosis (or borderline psychosis), especially those cases in which the process of individuation has made little progress and a strong "symbiotic" need has thus developed. But intense transference is by no means necessarily a symptom of severe mental disturbance. It also occurs frequently in cases of relatively minor disturbance. In these cases another factor can often be observed—namely, the infantilization of the patient produced by the arrangement used in the classic psychoanalytic procedure whereby the patient lies on a couch with the analyst sitting behind him, not responding to any direct questions but only voicing an "interpretation" from time to time. The patient tends to feel helpless in this situation, like a little child; and aroused in him are all the latent wishes to be attached to an idol.

This infantilization of the patient was not intended by Freud, at least not consciously. He offered other reasons for his procedure, such as his dislike of being "stared at" for hours by various patients. He also explained that the patient should not look at the analyst because he could thus more easily speak freely about embarrassing experiences; and that the patient should not be influenced by his observation of the analyst's reactions, such as changes in facial expression. I believe, however, that these reasons are largely rationalizations of the analyst's embarrassment about sharing with the patient the trip into the "underworld." He can listen to the patient's "bizarre" ideas, but to look at each other would make them embarrassingly real and destroy the borderline between what is "proper" and what is "improper." This peculiar attitude has its parallel in the fact that so many psychoanalysts, in their response to people and ideas outside the office, are often as blind and inauthentic as their more unenlightened fellow professionals.

Some analysts, such as R. Spitz, have clearly recognized that the real function of this arrangement is to infantilize the patient in order to produce a maximum of "childhood material." Having analyzed people for many years in the classic manner, and then later in a face-to-face situation, I observed that, especially in the less severe forms of mental disturbance, the intensity of the transference (not its existence) depends largely on the degree of this artificial infantilization. If the psychoanalyst responds to a patient as to another adult human being, if he does not hide himself behind the mask of "the great Unknown," and if the patient is given a more active role in the process, the intensity of the transference—as well as the obstacles created by this intensity—are considerably reduced.

Therapeutically speaking, the advantage of this latter procedure is that the patient's role as an adult person is not temporarily obliterated. He, the adult, is confronted with his unconscious strivings; and this confrontation is necessary if he is to react to, or even fully understand, the unconscious data. If the patient is therapeutically transformed into a child, the material he produces easily takes on the quality of experiences he had in a dream—something easily transformed into *memories* of unconscious desires, but without their being fully experienced. The oft-voiced idea that the patient will not express his most intimate (and often most embarrassing) thoughts in the face-to-face situation is erroneous. Those analysts who use this procedure have found that it is sometimes more difficult for the patient in the beginning, but that even the most embarrassing thoughts are expressed not less clearly in the face-to-face situation than on the couch. Moreover, once expressed, they are experienced with much greater reality than in the classic situation. In the latter case, the patient talks in an "interpersonal vacuum," and his thoughts often remain quite unreal to him; they gain full experiential reality only when they are truly shared with the analyst as a person, not as a shadowy phantom.

The crucial problem is how one interprets the transference—as a repetition of childhood experience, or as the mobilization of the ubiquitous desire for an idol?

The reasons for my assumption that the latter is the case were already implied in some of the foregoing remarks, where I stressed that one observes "transference" quite generally and without any connection to the psychoanalytic situation. But to this reasoning the objection can be made that one also finds in these situations that idol worship is the repetition of the relationship to mother and father. In answering this objection I can offer some observations. First of all, in those cases where a whole group is seized by the "idolatric passion," it exists regardless of the particular relationship to mother and father in each individual situation. Furthermore, I have found that there is no clear-cut correlation between childhood experience and the intensity of transference in the analytic situation. One can observe in a number of patients that intense transference is not paralleled by an equally intense early fixation to mother or father. Here I must emphasize that I do not mean to imply an absence of connection between the early and later experiences; indeed, in many cases such a connection can be seen clearly. Yet there are enough exceptions to suggest that the connection does not *necessarily* exist and, hence, that the classic assumption is an oversimplification. (Of course, if for dogmatic reasons one tends to read into every early fixation the intensity one observes clinically in transference, one can easily avoid the theoretical problem.)

In evaluating this problem one is fortunately not restricted to the type of idolatry that, when it occurs in the therapeutic situation, is labeled "transference." As I have indicated before, life is full of such "transferences." Much of what is known as "falling in love" and even enduring and intense relations in marriage and friendship are of the same type. In many such instances, only a distorted interpretation could make a case for an equally intense infantile fixation to be found in all cases. One can make similar observations in the context of individual reactions to a powerful leader. Common to such intense attachments is a more or less complete misconception about the real nature of the idol; and, again, there is no necessary connection with the corresponding relationship to one's parents.

A good example can be seen in the attachment of many leading Germans, both generals and civilians, to Hitler. From all descriptions it is evident that many were not acting principally out of fear. One can understand the blind obedience of these people, their deafness to their own consciences, their awe of Hitler, only by reference to the fact that they experienced him not as the real person (a destructive, clever, but immensely boring and banal petit-bourgeois with the cheap tastes of a nouveau riche), as many did after the catastrophe, but as a demigod, an all-powerful idol, charged with magic—whether black or white. Even while some plotted against him they were under his hypnotic influence. How is one to explain this? Could it be that all these people had a particular kind of father and were only repeating this early experience? No, it hardly seems likely that this should hold true for such a mixed group. Was it the result of abnormal insecurity? This, too, is not likely, inasmuch as the generals, especially, had been very successful under competitive conditions before. Was it a function of pure opportunism? This was indeed a factor in many cases, but it does not explain the intensity of the affective bond.

What else could it have been?

Hitler exhibited a somnambulistic certainty typical only of extremely narcissistic persons. His "magic" proceeded from his success during the first nine years of his reign (although this success was largely made possible by the money supplied by German industrialists, by the failure of Great Britain and France to contribute to his overthrow, and by the discord among and lack of courage of his opponents in Germany). Hitler was not interested in any human being; thus he was free of all warm sentiments. He could show an unrestricted aggressiveness against even his main collaborators, alternating this with friendly, benevolent smiles and gestures. In other words, through his behavior he made people feel like small children and offered himself as the all-knowing, all-powerful, all-punishing idol.

The recent book of memoirs by A. Speer, *Inside the Third Reich,* presents an abundance of material on the nature of this "transference." Speer was truly "in love" with Hitler until the day of Hitler's death. Even when doubts overcame him in the last years, and even though he counteracted Hitler's orders to destroy everything in Germany before leaving it to the enemy (Speer was apparently a biophilous person and not a necrophilous character like Hitler), Hitler retained the aura of an idol. Even at the end, when Hitler was powerless and sick, Speer's adoration remained. Yet from Speer's autobiography it becomes reasonably clear that his relationship to his father was not characterized by either excessive love or fear.

All these considerations invalidate neither Freud's concept of transference nor its tremendous significance. They simply lead to a wider definition: The transference phenomenon is to be understood as the expression of the fact that most men unconsciously feel like children and, hence, long for a powerful figure whom they can trust and to whom they can surrender. In fact, this is essentially what Freud indicated in *The Future of an Illusion* (1927c). The only difference between the view presented here and the classic theory is the idea that this longing is not necessarily—and is never exclusively—a repetition of childhood experience but, rather, is part of the "human condition."

The understanding of "transference" in the psychoanalytic situation is thus obscured if one focuses mainly on the relationship to mother and father, rather than considering it a human trait that is mobilized by certain later (acute or chronic) conditions and remains dependent on the total character structure of the person. It seems that Freud—under the influence of early clinical interpretations and, later, because of his acceptance of the idea of "repetition compulsion"—did not broaden his transference concept and hence did not apply it to some of the most widespread phenomena of human behavior. Here, as is so often the case with Freud's concepts, they have an even greater significance than he attributed to them if one liberates them from the limitations of the theoretical assumptions he made in his early clinical work.

I have not meant to imply that the need for idols is a fixed trait in human nature that cannot be overcome. Indeed, I have spoken of the "majority" of people and of the evidence in "past

51

or present history." But there have always been exceptional individuals who seem to have been free from the longing for idols. Besides, one can observe many individuals in whom the "idolatric passion," though present, is less strong than in the average person.

Overcoming the Fixation on Idols

The question, then, is what conditions account for the (relative) absence of the need for idols.

From what I have been able to observe over the many years during which this problem was central to my attention, I am led to this conclusion: The sense of powerlessness, and hence the need for idols, becomes less intense the more a person succeeds in attributing his existence to his own active efforts; the more he develops his powers of love and reason; the more he acquires a sense of identity, not mediated by his social role but rooted in the authenticity of his self; the more he can give and the more he is related to others, without losing his freedom and integrity; and the more he is aware of his unconscious, so that nothing human within himself and in others is alien to him.

What constitutes the individual conditions that have made it possible for some exceptional individuals to be free from idolatry is an issue so obviously complex that no attempt can be made here even to touch it. Yet great nonidolaters have certainly existed, and they have influenced the history of man decisively: Buddha, Isaiah, Socrates, Jesus, Meister Eckhart, Paracelsus, Boehme, Spinoza, Goethe, Marx, Schweitzer, and many others equally or less known that these. They were all "enlightened"; they could see the world as it is and were not afraid, knowing that man can be free if he is fully human. Some have expressed their faith in theistic terms; others have not. But for the former,

God had never become an idol. (Consider this statement by Meister Eckhart: "When I enter the ground, the bottom, the stream and the source of the Godhead, no one asks me where I came from or where I have been. No one missed me there, for there even God disappears" (Eckhart 1956, p. 182). They saw the truth and the truth made them free. They were filled with compassion, yet they were not sentimental; they showed great fortitude, yet also great tenderness. They descended into the abyss of their own souls, and ascended again to the light of the day. They needed no idol to save them because they rested on themselves; they had nothing to lose and had no goal except to achieve the fullest aliveness.

This kind of independence and enlightenment are rare, but there are many lesser degrees of independence and nonidolatry that are not. In such persons the idolatric passion, and their potential for forming "transferential" relationships, is slight. Life, to them, is a constant process of increasing the realm of freedom and nonidolatry.

Aside from individual constitution and childhood experiences, social conditions are of central importance if nonidolatry is to be more than an isolated phenomenon. These conditions are not difficult to describe; among the most important ones are absence of exploitation (hence also absence of the need for confusing the mind with justifying ideologies); the possibility for each person to be free from overt or hidden force and manipulation, beginning in early childhood; and stimulating influences that further the development of all a person's faculties. Wealth and a high consumption rate have nothing to do with freedom and independence. The "capitalist" and "communist" versions of industrial society are not conducive to the disappearance of the idolatric passion; on the contrary, they further it.

These thoughts on the helplessness of man and on the possibilities of overcoming it have been beautifully expressed by Freud:

> Thus I must contradict you when you go on to argue that men are completely unable to do without the consolation of the religious illusion, that without it they could not bear the troubles of life and the cruelties of reality. That is true, certainly, of the men into whom you have instilled the sweet—or bitter-sweet—poison from childhood onwards. But what of the other men, who have been sensibly brought up? Perhaps those who do not suffer from the neurosis will need no intoxicant to deaden it. They will, it is true, find themselves in a difficult situation. They will have to admit to themselves the full extent of their helplessness and their insignificance in the machinery of the universe; they can no longer be the centre of creation, no longer the object of tender care on the part of a beneficent Providence. They will be in the same position as a child who has left the parental house where he was so warm and comfortable. But surely infantilism is destined to be surmounted. Men cannot remain children for ever; they must in the end go out into the "hostile life." We may call this *"education to reality."* (Freud 1927c, p. 49; original emphasis)

The difference between this passage and the views expressed above is the following: Freud does not believe that the helplessness of man is largely the result of the irrational and opaque structure of his society, nor that in a society organized for the benefit of all, and transparent to all, his feeling of helplessness might be greatly reduced. In addition, Freud thinks only of the intellectual-scientific aspect that must develop if man is to achieve a greater degree of independence; he does not sufficiently take into consideration man's emotional development. In other words, and paradoxically, he does not connect one of his greatest clinical discoveries, transference, with his view of the infantile disposition in man and the possibilities of outgrowing it.

There is another aspect of unconsciousness, not related to the one just mentioned, with which the classic theory failed to come to grips. After all, there are quite a few contemporary human experiences that, by their very nature, cannot be explained in terms of the libido or the ego—for example, unconscious alienation, depression, the sense of lostness, powerlessness, and indifference to life. They are characteristic of life in the cybernated world and must be made accessible to analysis; but in the absence of a critical attitude toward society, they do not even become objects of psychoanalytic attention.

The Socially Repressed and Its Meaning for a Revision of the Unconscious

Another area in which much further work is needed is that of the unconscious and of repression. Although Freud gave up the "systematic" and topographical concept of the unconscious (*"Ucs."*) as theoretically unsatisfactory, the idea of "the unconscious" as a place or an entity remains central to psychoanalytic and popular thinking. (Many people use the term *subconscious,* which lends itself still better to the concept of a place.) However, there is no such thing or place as "the" unconscious (cf. Holt 1965). Unconsciousness is not a place but a *function.* I can be unaware of certain experiences (ideas, impulses) because strong defenses bar their entrance into consciousness. In this case these experiences can be said to be unconscious; or if not blocked, then they are conscious. (The terms *conscious* and *unconscious* are used here in Freud's dynamic sense, rather than in the descriptive sense that an idea is not in awareness at a given moment but can enter into awareness without difficulty.)

There are, of course, certain contents that tend to be more frequently unconscious than others, but this fact, too, does not support the topographical idea of a place called "the unconscious." The real question is why certain contents are repressed and what accounts for the respective difference in the severity of repression. There has been much discussion about the aggressive quality of the super-ego, linked to the death instinct, and metapsychological speculation about the respective roles of the ego and the super-ego in the process of repression. However, these speculations do not seem to cast much light on the clinical, observable phenomena; rather, they are abstract theoretical exercises that at best refine the theoretical formulation and at worst deflect from the examination of observable data, a great many more of which are necessary before this kind of theorizing can be very fruitful.

I want to mention here briefly one direction of investigation that, in my opinion, might be fruitfully followed—namely, the concept of the "social filter" (Fromm 1960a), which determines *which* experiences are permitted to arrive at consciousness. This "filter," consisting of language, logic, and mores (prohibited or permitted ideas and impulses), is of a social nature. It is specific to every culture and determines the "social unconscious," which in turn is rigidly prevented from reaching awareness because the repression of certain impulses and ideas has a very real and important function for the functioning of the society. Hence all of the cultural apparatus serves the purpose of keeping the social unconscious intact. It seems that individual repression, due to the particular experiences of the individual, is marginal by comparison, and, furthermore, that individual factors are all the more efficient when they operate in the same direction as the social factors. Whatever the merits of these concepts, a great deal of work will have to be done to build a more adequate theory of the social unconscious and its relation to the individual unconscious. (It hardly needs to be stated that the term *social unconscious,* as used here, has nothing to do with Jung's *collective unconscious;* the first deals with the social structure; the other, with archaic strivings common to all men.)

The same holds true for another line of thought that I have discussed in *The Forgotten Language* (Fromm 1951a). I refer to the view that the concepts of consciousness and unconsciousness are, strictly speaking, relative. What we usually call "consciousness" is a state of mind determined by our need to control nature for the aim of survival and, in the narrow sense, or for material production, to satisfy needs that have developed in the historical process. But we do not live only in order to take care of our biological needs and to protect ourselves against danger. In sleep—and, more rarely, in other states such as meditation and ecstasies or states induced by drugs—we are freed from the burden of taking care of survival; under these conditions another system of awareness can function in which we perceive ourselves and the world in an entirely subjective and personal way, without having to censor our awareness in the interests of survival-thinking. This mode of perception is conscious, for example, in our dreams. When we are asleep, the subjective experience is conscious and the "objective" experience is unconscious; and when we are awake, the opposite is the case.

Because the life of man has been devoted mainly to the fight for his existence, consciousness has been considered to be related exclusively to this purposive state of being. Complete freedom from external obligation, on the other hand, has been seen as unconscious. In fact, consciousness and the unconscious are entirely different modes of logic and experience, depending on the two different modes of being and acting. Only from the standpoint of common sense—that is, of the thinking related to practical action—do the processes of the "unconscious" appear as archaic, irrational, punitive. From the standpoint of freedom, they are not a bit less rational or unstructured than those of the consciousness.

The Dialectic Revision of Psychoanalysis

By studying this problem further, one will arrive, I believe, at a critical evaluation of Freud's concepts of "primary" and "secondary" processes, and of the traditional psychoanalytic investigation of artistic process, inasmuch as the latter is based on these concepts. (Unfortunately, classic psychoanalysis was greatly handicapped in developing a psychoanalytic theory of art because of the concept of "primary" process, which operates in the unconscious and by its very nature is an archaic, unstructured process within the id. Based on these premises, the language of art cannot be understood as what it is: another language, with its own logic and structure.)

One will be able to demonstrate (1) that various states of consciousness and unconsciousness, respectively, are determined by socioeconomic factors, specifically by the degree of preoccupation with the domination of nature, and (2) that the strict dichotomy between consciousness and unconsciousness is not necessary in individual or cultural constellations that are not dominated by interest in material production. When the balance has changed between the two states of being, their inherent antagonism is likely to disappear; then, as a consequence, it will be possible to talk about different forms of consciousness, each with its own structure and logic, and about the possibility of their being blended with each other.

An entirely different area of unconsciousness to be studied is that of "false consciousness." I am referring to the fact that we conceive of ourselves, of others, and of situations in a distorted (false) "way," and that we are unaware of what they really are— or, more precisely, of what they are not. The child in the fairy tale about the emperor's clothes is aware of what the emperor is not; he is not clothed. Our own inner needs, combined with social suggestion, almost never adequately inform us as to what a person or a situation is not. We fail to see, for example, that our actions are not in accordance with our values, that our leaders are not different from the average man, that we ourselves are not fully awake, are not making sense, are not happy. We are not aware that love and freedom are abstractions, that we cannot "have" them but, rather, can only love and liberate ourselves—which we are not doing. Although awareness of what we are not is less frightening than awareness of the chaotic unconscious described before, it is still very uncomfortable. Unconsciousness is identical with unawareness of truth; becoming aware of the unconscious means discovering the truth. This concept of truth is not the traditional one of the correspondence between thought and that to which thought refers; rather, it is a dynamic one, in which truth is the process of removing illusions, of recognizing what the object is *not*. Truth is not a final statement about something but a step in the direction of undeception (Ent-taüschung); awareness of the unconscious becomes an essential element of truth-seeking, education a process of de-deception.

What is normally unconscious in the waking mind is made conscious in art. The poet expresses that experience which the average person senses but is unconscious of; by giving it form he is able to communicate the experience to others. The dramatist gives life to an experience that is normally repressed because it contradicts all permissible experience. If Hamlet had come to a psychoanalyst he probably would have complained about an "uneasy feeling" when he was with his mother and an "unreasonable distrust of his stepfather"; he probably would have added that "these feelings are quite neurotic, given that, in reality, his mother and stepfather are very decent people and quite kind to him." A classic analyst might then have tried to show him that his hatred of his uncle was the result of his Oedipus-rivalry, and that the root of the whole complex lay in his incestuous desire for his mother. Shakespeare's analysis, on the other hand, consists in uncovering Hamlet's unconscious insight into the real character of his mother and uncle: They are ruthless, lying murderers. What Hamlet represses is not his incestuous desire but his awareness of reality. And the device of the ghost serves to establish the truth of Hamlet's suspicions.

The artist unveils the truth, which is repressed because it is incompatible with convention and the "thinkable." In his art he does what the psychoanalyst does on a private scale: He uncovers the repressed truth. For this reason all great art is revolutionary. Even the "reactionary" artist (e.g., Dostoevski) is a revolutionary because he uncovers the hidden truth, whereas the "artist" of "socialist realism" is reactionary because he helps to protect state-made illusions. Homer's description of the Trojan War did more for peace than did the peace "art" used by political propaganda.

The New Concept of the Unconscious According to Ronald D. Laing

Profound new insights into the understanding of unconscious processes have made their appearance in R. D. Laing's work (cf. Laing 1960, 1961, 1964, 1964a, 1966, and 1967). Technically speaking, Laing represents "existentialist psychoanalysis" (cf. May et al. 1958); but aside from some general philosophical positions he shares with other existentialists, his approach is distinguished by deep penetration into each detail of the patient's fantasies and behavior as well as by his concern and empathy. This is an approach very different from the one shown, for instance, in the case history of Ellen West by one of the founders of existential analysis, Ludwig Binswanger. Binswanger (though this is by no means true of all existentialist psychoanalysts) does not enter into an understanding of the life experience of the patient, but simply gives a very conventional report and then labels the various symptoms, complexes, and desires, with terms drawn from E. Husserl's and M. Heidegger's vocabularies. The patient remains unknown, and nothing is really revealed except an array of philosophical phrases, hiding a conventional and alienated approach.

Laing is first of all a radical humanist. Characteristic of this aspect of his position is the statement:

> Humanity is estranged from its authentic possibilities. This basic vision prevents us from taking any unequivocal view of the sanity of common sense, or of the madness of the so-called madmen. . . . Our alienation goes to the roots. The realization of this is the essential springboard for any serious reflection on any aspect of present interhuman life. Viewed from different perspectives, construed in different ways and expressed in different idioms, this realization unites men as diverse as Marx, Kierkegaard, Nietzsche, Freud, Heidegger, Tillich and Sartre.

Closely related to Laing's humanist position is his concept of therapy as expressed in the following statement: "Psychotherapy must remain *an obstinate attempt of two people to recover the wholeness of being human through the relationship between them*" (Laing 1967a, p. 34. Emphasis added). He states that "a therapeutic relationship with an object-to-be-changed rather than a person-to-be-accepted, simply perpetuates the disease it purports to cure" (Laing 1967a, p. 32).

Laing's most original contributions concern the unconscious aspects of a person's experience. In *The Self and Others*, he presents a most penetrating analysis of phenomena that have been neglected by most psychoanalysts. Within the history of psychoanalytic thought, Laing's thinking is in my opinion closely related to the thought of H. S. Sullivan. In saying this I refer to his concrete description of the patient's unconscious fantasies and communications with others, specifically with the analyst as a "participant observer." Suffice it to say here that he has cast new light on the interpersonal experiences of the schizophrenic patient, not only by describing what goes on in him as a man suffering from schizophrenia but also by describing the interpersonal communication within his family. In addition to the data on schizophrenic experience, Laing has analyzed a number of other most relevant experiences; his discussion of the phenomena of "fantasy," "pretense," and the "elusion of experience," of "identity" and the experience of self, of "confirmation," "dis-conformation," and "collusion," are particularly worthy of mention. The significance of Laing's approach for the creative revision of psychoanalysis lies in the depth of his experience of life and in his application of the principle of minute observation and description, unhampered by the ballast of dogmatic thinking and free from conventional repression by his critical approach to existing society. (Cf. Laing 1961, p. 63.) In only one essential respect do I have to disagree with Laing. He takes the position that there is no "basic personality" or "one internal system" but, rather, that every person causes within himself "various internalized social modes of being." He also holds that there are no "basic" emotions, instincts, or personality outside of the relationship a person has within one or another social context (Laing 1967a, pp. 66–67).

I only want to say that the assumption of a basic character system in person A does not exclude the possibility that this system is constantly being affected by systems B, C, D, . . . with which it communicates, and that in this interpersonal process various aspects of the character system in person A are energized and others lose in intensity. The simplest example is the person characterized by a sadomasochistic system. In his encounter with one system (B) his sadism will be activated; in his encounter with another (C) his masochism will be activated. However, the person in whose system sadomasochism is not pronounced will react neither masochistically nor sadistically when he encounters systems B or C, respectively.

Laing has discussed the problem of adjustment and adaptation from a radical humanist and sociocritical position: "If the formation is itself off course, then the man who is really to get on course must leave the formation" (Laing 1967a, p. 82).

But perhaps his greatest achievement thus far is what one could conventionally call his "contribution to the study of schizophrenia." This, however, would be a very poor way of describing Laing's approach, because, from his perspective, this "illness" ceases to be an illness and becomes a state of being, a journey into the darkness of the inner world, a dimension of being in comparison to which the "normal" ego experience is a preliminary illusion. What Laing has to say here goes far beyond what, to my knowledge, has been said by psychoanalysts thus far; and it opens up new vistas for the psychoanalytic understanding not only of psychosis but also of the "normal" mind (in both its healthy and its sick aspects) and of religious and artistic experience. His work, in my opinion, is the most important and promising contribution to the dialectic revision of psychoanalysis.

Causes of Overcoming Repression

In addition to learning the causes of repression it is equally important to discover the factors that permit and further de-repression, by which the unconscious becomes conscious. This, after all, is the key to psychoanalytic therapy, but it has attracted relatively little attention. For an explanation people were all too ready to rely on the traditional psychoanalytic answer that suffering from the symptom, on the one hand, and having a positive transference relationship to the analyst, on the other, are largely responsible for de-repression. This is undoubtedly true, but it is not a sufficient explanation for the occurrence of de-repression in therapeutic situations. (In my experience the strength of the biophilous tendencies in comparison with necrophilous ones plays a decisive role as a condition for de-repression.)

The question must be raised regardless of whether awareness of the unconscious is possible only as a result of psychoanalytic therapy. Does it happen outside of this situation? And if so what are the important factors? The dialectic revision of psychoanalysis will focus on this problem, and many new insights are to be expected from such research.

I want to mention here only a few factors that appear relevant to me. One is social: It seems that situations of radical social change, in which many traditional categories of thinking and feeling begin to crumble, are conducive to de-repression, at least in certain areas. Another factor seems to be the degree of "awakeness" or aliveness of a person. Though difficult to describe, "awakeness" is an experience of which many people sensitive to their moods are aware. They discover differences of awakeness in themselves in different states of being, and they can make the same observation in others. They might find that most people can actually be considered half-asleep relative to the state of greater awakeness that is possible. The reasons for this lie to a large extent in the semi-hypnotic dependence of such people on the suggestive influence of leaders, slogans, and so on. Another reason is the obsessional busy-ness of people, which not only prevents them from ever "coming to themselves" but also reduces their awakeness to the level necessary for going about their business. The practices of physical and mental relaxation, of silence and concentration, seem to be conducive to reaching a higher level of awakeness and hence awareness.

It seems to me that the idea, so fashionable today, that people can discover their unconscious by talking "frankly" about themselves in a group is based on an illusion. To say frankly what one thinks and feels about oneself and others usually produces not unconscious material but conscious (though secret and not usually communicated) material. By sharing it with others, one tends to miss the truly unconscious components, which are subtle enough that the crude instruments of group-talk will tend to hide them rather than revealing them. Quite the contrary, I believe that by being silent and concentrated, and by wishing to bring the unconscious to consciousness, one is probably more successful than by constantly talking with others. The ideal solution seems to be the possibility of communicating with another person in a quiet way, such that the listener—if he says anything at all—raises some questions and tries to communicate what he understands of the unconscious communication. This is what the situation of psychoanalytic therapy ought to be.

THE RELEVANCE OF SOCIETY, SEXUALITY, AND THE BODY IN A REVISED PSYCHOANALYSIS

Freud clearly recognized the connection between individual and society, and hence the fact that individual and social psychology are intertwined. But by and large he tended to explain social structure as determined by instinctive needs rather than emphasizing their interaction. It was unavoidable that psychoanalysts should become increasingly interested in the application of psychoanalytic findings to social data. These attempts were made from the anthropological standpoint by Freud himself, in *Totem and Tabu*. G. Roheim analyzed his anthropological data on the basis of Freud's theory. A. Kardiner, in collaboration with anthropologists, attempted an understanding of the "basic personality" of primitive society. And with respect to the analysis of sociological data, the earliest attempts were made by W. Reich and myself.

Whereas Reich focused on the relationship among sexual morality, repression, and society, I was mainly interested in the "social character"—that is, the "character matrix" shared by the members of a society and class, through which general human energy is transformed into the special human energy necessary for the functioning of a given society.

As the growing social and human crisis has made clear, in order to understand such phenomena as war, aggression, alienation, apathy, and the consumption compulsion, one has to arrive at a better understanding of the unconscious aspects of human motivation and the way in which it interacts with socioeconomic and political forces. A number of contributions have been made by writers who, though not psychoanalysts themselves, have used psychoanalytic concepts; among them are D. Riesman in his work on the American character (1950) and H. Marcuse in his studies on the effects of a "repressive" society on sexuality and Eros (1966).

I have pursued my own research on social character mainly in *Escape from Freedom* (1941a), *The Sane Society* (1955a), and two large empirical studies, *The Working Class in Weimar Germany* (on the authoritarian character of German workers and employees [1980a]) and, with M. Maccoby, on *Social Character in a Mexican Village* (1970b). I am convinced that further research in the field of analytic social psychology can greatly contribute to the identification of pathological elements in a sick society as well as of the pathogenic social factors that produce and increase the "pathology of normalcy."

The study of sexuality has not been given sufficient attention in classic psychoanalysis. At first glance this statement might appear to be absurd, or paradoxical: Did not Freud build his whole theory of drives on the concept of sexuality?

A more thorough investigation of Freud's writings, psychoanalytic literature, and orthodox psychoanalytic practice reveals that sexuality is treated in a somewhat abstract or schematic way. The child is supposed to pass through the libidinous phases; the adult can be fixated in one such phase (or be regressed to it), but there is a certain lack of interest in the many concrete and specific facets of sexual, especially genital, behavior. Although A. C. Kinsey and W. W. Masters have presented us with a wealth of data about sexual behavior (but little insight into their psychological meaning), the psychoanalytic literature has not produced any comparable body of clinical data. This seems partly due to a certain reluctance to talk too frankly about sexual practices—a reluctance one can find not only in Freud (though understandable in view of his background) but also in most of his disciples, who possessed a conventional sense of prudishness on these matters.

The revision of thought on sexuality will have to put much greater emphasis on the concrete details of sexual behavior and the understanding of them. This refers above all to "normal" sexual behavior. It is not enough to state that a man or a woman has an orgasm in the crude and insufficient terms of what Kinsey calls an "outlet"; rather, one must understand the *quality* of the orgastic experience. The most important step in this direction was taken by W. Reich, who considered the relaxation of the whole body a condition for full "orgastic potency" and, in general, for a relaxed attitude, in contrast to the bodily "armor" that is related to repression and resistance. It should be added that Reich's concept of orgastic potency led eventually beyond the problem of purely somatic relaxation. Ambition, envy, anger, avarice, greed (the classical sins, but also, in Freudian terminology, the outcomes of pregenital strivings) block full relaxation.

The "spiritual" problem of *being* as against the passion for *having* cannot be separated from that of full relaxation.

Furthermore, especially in view of the growing tendency to extend equality to *sameness* between the sexes, we need to study the phenomenon of "erotic sexuality" (rooted in the male-female polarity) as against "nonerotic" sexuality based on the desire for physical de-tension and body proximity. In the latter type of sexuality, the difference between homo- and heterosexuality are somewhat blurred and, on the whole, constitute a blending between the psychic characteristics of infantile sexuality and the characteristics of adult physiology.

The other aspects of sexuality in need of revision are the sexual "abnormalities," especially the perversions. Here, too, a facile explanation in theoretical terms has obscured the reality. We must ask the question: What is the quality of bodily and mental experience in perversions in comparison to that in genital sexual intercourse? Furthermore, what relationship do the perversions have to the character of the person—outside of the sphere of sex? Is the sadistic man who is excited only when he inflicts pain and humiliation on a woman characterologically affected by this sadistic craving in his ordinary life? Or is his sexual sadism rooted in his sadistic character? And what is the psychological difference between oral and anal perversions? Many more important questions in this context need to be studied; but this can be done only if sexuality is no longer treated so cautiously and so theoretically.

The understanding of the body as a way of understanding the unconscious has been left completely untouched by the classic theory. One aspect of this understanding is a theoretical one, whereby the body is "a symbol of the soul"; the formation of the body, the posture, the gait, the gestures, the facial expressions, the way of breathing and talking tell as much, or more, about the unconscious of a person than almost any other data traditionally used in the psychoanalytic process.

Not only a person's character (especially in its unconscious aspects) but also important aspects of neurotic disturbances are visible in his bodily movements. One of the most important contributions of Reich was to have seen the connection between bodily posture and resistance on the one hand, and bodily relaxation, de-repression, and health on the other.

Whatever the merits of Reich's later theories on the "orgon," and so on, his emphasis on bodily processes as an expression of the unconscious should, in my opinion, be counted among the most important contributions to psychoanalytic theory. Of course, his point of view was so much in contrast to that of the majority of psychoanalysts, for whom words and theoretical concept were the main concern, that one can understand why his ideas were not well received by them. Only a small group of adherents took them seriously. Reich's work did influence others, who developed his point of view creatively. I will mention here only one author: B. Christiansen (1963), who wrote a most interesting work dealing with this area: *Thus Speaks the Body: Attempts Toward a Personology from the Point of View of Respiration and Postures.* Outside the psychoanalytic field, the psychological importance of bodily relation was stressed by I. H. Schultz, whose autogenic training was widely influential and stimulated other psychiatrists in the elaboration of non-auto-suggestive methods of bodily relaxation. In the last few decades, insight into the psychological value of bodily relaxation has been greatly enhanced by increasing acquaintance with the various Yoga systems, as well as by their Western counterparts in the systems of E. Gindler, made popular in the United States by Charlotte Selver and others. I believe that we are only on the threshold of a most important field of theory-therapy, characterized by an emphasis on awareness of experience, rather than on thinking about experience. I also believe that a creative development of psychoanalysis will lead to new important findings in this area.

THE REVISION OF PSYCHOANALYTIC THERAPY

Aspects in the Realm of Therapeutic Practice

The need for a revision of psychoanalytic therapy is recognized by many analysts; the question is only how deep a revision is envisaged. In the writings of Sullivan, Laing, myself, and others, the most fundamental point of a revision is the transformation of the whole analytic situation from one in which a detached observer studies an "object" to one of interpersonal communication. This is possible only if the analyst responds to the patient, who in turn responds to the analyst's response, and so on. In this process the analyst becomes aware of experiences that at a given moment the patient may not be aware of; and by communicating what he sees, the analyst furthers new responses. The whole process leads to ever-greater clarification.

All this is possible only if the analyst experiences within himself what goes on in the patient and does not approach him merely cerebrally—if he sees and sees and sees, and thinks as little as is absolutely necessary and, furthermore, if he gives up the illusion that he is "well" and the patient is "sick." They are both human, and if the experience of the patient, even the sickest patient, fails to strike a chord of experience within the analyst, he does not understand the patient.

The analyst has the patient's genuine confidence only if he permits himself to be vulnerable and does not hide behind the role of a professional man who knows the answers because he is paid for knowing the answers. The fact is that he and the patient are engaged in a common task—the shared understanding of the patient's experience, and of the analyst's response to his experience—not of the patient's "problem"; the patient *has* no problem but *is* a person who is suffering from his way of being.

Another respect in which I believe a revision of therapy is necessary concerns the significance of childhood. Classic analysis is prone to see in the present "nothing but" the repetition of the past (i.e., early childhood), and its concept of therapy is to bring the infantile conflict into awareness so that the strengthened ego of the patient can better cope with the repressed instinctual material than the child was able to do. Because Freud recognized that in many (if not most) cases, the original infantile experience is not remembered, he expected to find it in a "new edition," as it were, of the data brought to light by the observation of transference.

Many analysts began to rely on reconstructions of what had "probably" happened in childhood; they assumed that if the patient understood *why* he had become the way he is, this very insight would cure him. However, reconstructed knowledge has no curative effect and is nothing but the intellectual acceptance of real or alleged facts and theories. Of course, if the suggestion is given overtly or implicitly that the knowledge of these facts will cure the symptom, the power of suggestion—as in the case of exorcising the devil—may produce a "cure," albeit not an analytic one. That the conditions for suggestibility are enhanced in the artificially infantilizing situation of the patient vis à vis the analyst in the classic procedure can hardly be contested. Thus psychoanalytic therapy has often deteriorated into a mere probing into a patient's past, without leading to the experience of uncovering the repressed.

A further consequence of this method is that it has led to a mechanical translation of every recent person in touch with the patient into father, mother, or some other significant person of his childhood, rather than to an understanding of the quality and function of the patient's experience. A man may tend to feel envious of his colleagues—for example, see them as a threat to his security or success—and become seriously disturbed by the constant need to fight his rivals. And the analyst may be prone to explain this as a repetition of his jealousy of a brother, and to believe that this interpretation will cure the patient's feelings of rivalry. But even assuming that the patient can remember the jealousy he felt for his brother, the analysis is by no means finished at this point. What is still needed is to understand in detail the exact quality of his experience of jealousy, both in childhood and today. He will then become aware of many unconscious aspects of his past or present experience, having to do with his sense of unmanliness, for instance, or his impotence, his dependence on protective figures, his narcissism, his fantasies of grandeur—as the case may be. It will become clear that his rivalry is to be understood not as a repetition but as an outcome of a whole *system,* of which the rivalry is one element.

One must keep in mind that the aim of psychoanalytic therapy is not historical research into early childhood as an end in itself but, rather, the uncovering of what is unconscious. Much of what is unconscious now was unconscious early in life, and much has become unconscious a great deal later. It is not the past in itself that is interesting for psychoanalysis but the past inasmuch as it is present. By looking mainly at the past and expecting the present to be its repetition, one tends to oversimplify and to ignore the fact that much of what appears to be repetition is not—that what is repressed now is a whole system, as "secret plot" that determines a person's life, and not single experience entities such as castration fear, mother attachment, and so on.

Even if it were possible to recover all repressed childhood experiences, one would have uncovered a considerable part of the unconscious—but by no means all of it, inasmuch as many repressions took place later on. (This is the genetic approach.) On the other hand, if one knew nothing about these childhood experiences, one could discover all that is repressed by taking the equivalent of an X-ray picture—that is, by studying the "present" unconscious via the transference phenomena, dreams, associations, slips, style of speaking, gestures, movements, facial expressions, tone of voice; in short, all manifestations of behavior. (This is the functional approach.) (Note especially that the transference phenomena are much more than the experiences of childhood, in relation to father and mother, that are now transferred.)

Both the genetic and functional approaches are legitimate. However, if one uses only the genetic approach and transference (as mere repetition of childhood experience), one not only misses a great deal of unconscious material but is also prone to use the discovery of the childhood material for the purpose of explaining *why* the patient has become the person he currently is. In doing so, one has changed the central psychoanalytic principle of *experiencing* the unconscious into historical research. And though this may be good (but not good enough) for purposes of the psychobiography of a person, it is of no therapeutic value. Many psychoanalytic patients and analysts are satisfied when the analysis has resulted in what appears to be a satisfactory *explanation* of their neurosis in a purely intellectual rather than experiential manner. (I am, of course, aware of the fact that most analysts emphasize that analysis should not be only a cerebral experience; I am referring not to this theoretical postulate but to what I have observed goes on in practice in many instances.)

These brief remarks will become more meaningful if one recalls what has been said earlier about the fixation to mother and father: that the longing for these figures is only partly explained as a repetition of earlier ties, but is rooted in the total psychic structure of a person unless he has become fully himself.

Of course, classic analysts are right in criticizing a superficial or simply educational approach to the present, but they are quite wrong regarding the functional approach in the sense mentioned here. There is nothing superficial about delving into the deeply repressed aspects of the present experience, whereas the purely cerebral approach to childhood material can be very superficial. Our knowledge of these problems is very inadequate; and, in my opinion, much effort is necessary to arrive at a sounder insight into the curative role of recall, re-experience, and reconstruction of childhood experience.

Such studies should examine another closely related problem about which we know next to nothing. I am referring to the theories about the connection between early and later experience. According to classic theory, the later experience is a repetition of an earlier one by way of fixation on, or regression to, certain pregenital levels of libido, assuming a causal nexus between past and present. For example, the miser is supposed to have regressed to the anal level of libido development. However, as I have already pointed out, what we are dealing with in anal-hoarding, in the oral-sadistic (exploitative) orientation, in sadism and masochism, in biophilia and necrophilia, in narcissism and incestuous fixation, are ways of life that reflect the effort, however desperate, to cope with the fundamental question posed by human experience. One of these solutions may be better than another from the standpoint of the most harmonious and vital experience of life, but they all fulfill the function of a system of orientation and devotion. They are all "spiritual orientations" in the sense of the definition given above. A person adapts one of these orientations as his private religion, as it were, and lives in accordance with it. And the orientation is powerful, not because it entails regression to a pregenital level of libido but because it fulfills the function of being an answer to life endowed with the energy of the whole system.

What accounts for the person's specific orientation? Aside from constitutional factors, the answer would seem to be the social character of the society in which he lives and, to a smaller degree, the specific variation of the family he has been born into. The implication here is that we understand character development essentially as a response of man to the total configuration of the society of which he is a part, mediated originally through his family. One might hypothesize that infancy and early childhood permit the "practice" of various forms of orientation because they are suggested by the stages of the body's development. The early biological stages, however, are not necessarily the *cause* of the later development but, rather, only the *first instance* of a character formation molded by interpersonal factors that manifest themselves from childhood on throughout life—that is, unless new and counteracting forces are set in motion, among them the force of awareness.

Transtherapeutic Aspects of Psychoanalysis

Let me add one final but extremely important point in regard to the revision of the theory and practice of psychoanalytic therapy, which, as I have pointed out, started out as a method to cure neurotic illness in the traditional meaning of the word. It then proceeded to treat the "neurotic character"—that is, a character system that was considered sick, although it did not have conventional symptoms. More and more, psychoanalysis was sought by people who were unhappy and dissatisfied with their lives, by people who felt anxious, empty, and without joy. Although the reason for their treatment was "rationalized" in the traditional terms of being cured of chronic illness, the fact was that many were seeking a higher degree of well-being. They wanted to "express their potentialities," to be able to love fully, to overcome their narcissism or their hostility; and even if they did not come to the analyst with a clear awareness of these goals, it soon became evident that this was the real reason for their seeking analytic help.

What is a "therapy" whose gain is greater joy and vitality, greater awareness of self and others, greater capacity to love, greater independence and freedom to be oneself? It is, indeed, no longer a "therapy"—at least not in the traditional sense of the word—but a method for human growth, a "therapy of the soul," as in the literal translation of psychotherapy.

In this type of psychoanalysis, personal problems, like insomnia, or unhappy relations with spouse or children are looked upon not as the final problems to be solved but as indications of a generally unsatisfactory state of existence. It becomes clear, in fact, that none of these "problems" can really be solved unless a radical change takes place in the whole person.

Something else becomes clear, too. No change in state of mind and experience is possible unless it is accompanied by a change in one's practice of life. To give a simple example: If a son fixated to his mother has become aware of this fixation and its roots, the awareness in itself will not become effective unless the son changes those practices in his life that are expressions of, and simultaneously feed, this fixation. The same holds true for a man who holds a job that forces him into continuous submission and/or insincerity. No insight will work unless he gives up this job, even if material or other sacrifices result. It is precisely this necessity to make certain relevant painful changes in one's practice of life that makes success in therapy so difficult.

Psychoanalysis as a "therapy of the soul" has by no means superseded its older role as a therapy against illness. A number of therapeutic methods have been found that can cure certain symptoms more adequately and/or more quickly than psychoanalysis, but many pathological manifestations remain, from mild to severe, for which psychoanalysis is the only available form of therapy. (Even the fact that certain forms of mental illness are cured only in a minority of cases is not an argument against the value of psychoanalysis as long as no other or better method is known.) In many instances, the cure of symptoms is possible without reaching the depth of a patient's personality (the latter being the condition for the "cure of the soul"). But the understanding and changing of the psychotic person, as well as of the "neurotic character," are impossible if the deepest layers of the person's existence are not touched.

This spiritual experience, which underlies many theistic and nontheistic forms of union and at-onement, is closely related to the problem of sanity. Human existence is an absurdity; it would be impossible to experience fully the dichotomy of human existence and to remain sane. "Sanity" is "normalcy" paid for by the anesthetizing of full awareness by false consciousness, routine busy-ness, duty, suffering, and so on. Most people live by successful compensation for their potential insanity and thus are sane for all practical purposes—that is, for the purposes of physical and social survival. However, when any part of their compensation is threatened, the potential insanity may become manifest. For this reason any attack on compensatory ideas, figures, or institutions constitutes a serious threat and is reacted to by intense aggression.

There is only one way to overcome this potential insanity: by achieving full awareness of ourselves. This requires that we be in touch with the archaic, irrational forces within ourselves, as well as with those with which we are pregnant and to which we have not yet given birth; it requires that we experience the murderer, the insane person, and the saint within ourselves and within others. Under these conditions, when there is no need for repression, the possibility exists for emergence of the self as the integrating subject of authentic being, in contrast to the ego as the object that one "has." (*Ego* is used here in the popular rather than technical sense of psychoanalysis.) In being, there is nothing to hold on to and, hence, nothing to be afraid of. It is the I who can say, along with Goethe, "I have placed my house on nothing—therefore the whole world belongs to me." Then life cannot elude one, for "the life I am trying to grasp is the me that is trying to grasp it" (Laing 1967a, p. 156).

Our categories of "reality" are not just so many illusions; they are necessary if we want to survive and live. In fact, they constitute the basis for any experience, including that of dying. The "sane" person is faced with this difficulty: that if he has had a glimpse of his own depth, an experience of extraordinary perception transcending the conventional one, he tends to be frightened and to cover up what he has experienced, to forget it, and perhaps to remember it in an intellectual, nonexperiential way.

There are many methods of achieving this goal of enlightenment. But the problem in all these methods is that of attaining a new experience of depth without getting lost in the labyrinth of one's "underworld" and becoming incapable of seeing the world and others as they must be seen if one wants to live. I refer here to the sociobiological need of man to work in order to live—that is, to the need to be able to see the "outer" world in a frame of reference that makes it "manageable." This problem relates not to the *cultural* determination of our perception, which varies from culture to culture, but to a *frame of reference to be found in all cultures,* in which fire is fire that can harm and can warm, contrary to the love or passion that it is in the "inner" world.

There is still another aspect to the danger of descending into the labyrinth. This experience, in whatever way it is produced—

for example, through meditation, autosuggestion, or drugs—can lead to a state of narcissism in which nobody and nothing else exist outside of the expanded self. This state of mind is egoless inasmuch as the person has lost his ego as something to hold onto; but it can nevertheless be a state of intense narcissism in which there is no relatedness to anyone, inasmuch as there is no one, outside of the extended self. This type of mystical experience has been misunderstood by Freud and many others as representing mystical experience as such (the "Oceanic feeling") and has been interpreted by Freud as regression to primary narcissism.

But there is another type of mystical experience that is not narcissistic, which is found in Buddhist, Christian, Jewish, and Muslim mysticism. The difference is not easily discovered, because the formulations of the experience in both types are very much alike. In fact, the difference can be inferred only from what is known about the personality of the mystic, and to some extent from his total philosophy. Nevertheless, it is very real and very important; for narcissistic egolessness, like narcissism in general, constitutes a crippled state of being.

Among many answers to the problem of how to attain enlightenment without becoming insane or entering a state of primary narcissism, the most systematic and brilliant is perhaps the practice of Zen Buddhism. Its view of the solution is suggested by the following saying: "First mountains are mountains and rivers are rivers; then mountains are not mountains and rivers are not rivers; eventually, mountains are mountains and rivers are rivers." The same concept in a nonparadoxical form was once expressed by the late Daisetz Suzuki: "One who is enlightened walks on the ground, except that he is a few inches above it" (personal communication, 1957). Besides, the principle of compassion, central in all Buddhist thinking, tends to prevent the narcissistic type of mystical experience.

The Dialectic Revision of Psychoanalysis

What has psychoanalysis to do with the attainment of such experience? I believe that it can be an approach to enlightenment—one perhaps particularly suited to the Western mind. It allows us to experience the depth of our own "underworld" (Freud's "acheronta"), first under the guidance of an analyst who can encourage his analysand to descend deeper because he will not leave him alone on his voyage, and later through continuous self-analysis. Self-awareness, decreasing defensiveness, diminishing greed, and increasing self-activation may be steps toward enlightenment if they are combined with other practices such as meditation and concentration, and if the person makes a great effort. "Instant enlightenment" with the aid of drugs, however, is no substitute for a radical change of personality. How far one will go depends on many circumstances. Attainment of the goal is extremely difficult, but many steps can be taken toward it. In fact, the "goal" should be forgotten as another "accomplishment" to which one is greedily attached. Although our subject is not psychoanalysis as a means of furthering spiritual development, the point is important enough to be mentioned, albeit sketchily, in this outline of a program for dialectic revision.

These considerations may seem to be far removed from the method by which Freud tried to cure hysterical and obsessional patients. But if we remember his interest in a movement that was to lead men to an optimum of awareness and reason, the idea of psychoanalysis as a method for spiritual cure, though quite in contrast to Freud's rationalistic assumptions, may nevertheless be in contact with the deepest concern of its founder: not only to cure illness but to find a way to "well-being."

3

Sexuality and
Sexual Perversions

ASPECTS OF THE SEXUAL LIBERATION MOVEMENT

One of the most profound changes to have occurred, at an accelerating pace, within the last ten to twenty years (and in a broader sense since the 1920s) has been the change in ideas and practices with respect to sexuality—a change so drastic that we can speak of a sexual revolution or of a movement for the liberation of sex. In the most general terms, this movement can be characterized by the claim that sexual pleasure is a legitimate aim in itself and does not need any justification by the intention—or objective possibility—of procreation as a concomitant of the sexual act. Sexual enjoyment is considered an inalienable and unconditional right of any human being.

This change in attitude implies the repudiation of the traditional Christian position and especially that of the Roman Catholic Church, for which the "natural" purpose is "unnatural" (in the sense of the divine plan) and sinful, to be compared with the masturbatory practice of Onan. The sexual liberation movement began on a somewhat limited scale among the younger generation of the 1920s, and in the 1950s and 1960s became a mass phenomenon in North America and most European countries. The force of this movement finds a telling expression in the widespread dissent over the anti-pill ruling of Pope Paul VI among millions of people who cannot be considered in any way radical or rebellious.

If one thus defines the sexual revolution in terms of affirmation of the right to sexual pleasure or happiness, it seems part and parcel of the general trend toward liberalization and greater freedom that characterizes the political development of the Western countries—a development that could be characterized as historically logical and progressive. However, a few questions arise that indicate the problem is not that simple. First, is it valid to speak of an increasing tendency toward personal freedom within the Western world? Or is this statement an ideological one, in contrast to the fact of increasing conformity and alienation? And are such widespread practices as promiscuity and "multi-sex" among the middle-aged members of the middle class and the younger ones in all classes a sign that the society has achieved a greater degree of spontaneity and freedom?

It seems that the people practicing the new sexual mores are otherwise very well adapted to the dominant social patterns of thinking and feeling and by no means a radical avant-garde. Can the sexual revolution among these well-adjusted members of our alienated society really be called a revolution or liberation when their lives are still so deeply conventional? And is the sexual behavior of the hippies and of leftist students part of the same phenomenon? The following discussion attempts to answer these questions.

Sexuality and Consumerism

An analysis of the social psychological development during the last fifty years reveals the existence of two entirely different trends. The most noticeable is the growth of the consumer attitude. The economic requirements for capital accumulation in the nineteenth century required of the middle-class man that he develop a character for which saving and hoarding was an inner need, the fulfillment of which satisfied him; and the necessities of the cybernated mass-producing society in the beginning of the second industrial revolution required a personality who found his satisfaction in spending and consuming. Thus man was transformed into a busy but inwardly passive *homo consumens*. The motto of this new type of man was expressed tellingly by A. Huxley in his *Brave New World* (1946): "Never put off till tomorrow the fun you can have today."

What is essential for modern consumption is that it be perceived as an attitude or, to put it more correctly, as a character trait. It does not matter *what* one consumes; it can be food, drink, television, books, cigarettes, painting, music, or sex. The world in its richness is transformed into an object of consumption. In the act of consuming the person is passive, greedily sucking the object of his consumption while at the same time being sucked in by it. The objects of consumption lose their concrete qualities because they are sought after not by specific and real human faculties but by one powerful striving: the greed to have and to use. Consumption is the alienated form of being in contact with the world by making the world an object of one's greed rather than an object of one's interest and concern.

If the economic system requires a social character whose aim is consumption, it can hardly keep up a Victorian morality: One cannot produce consumption-addicts and train them at the same time to be hoarders and to repress their greed with regard to ever-present (actual or potential) sexual desires. Sexual consumption shares the quality of all consumption; it is shallow, impersonal, lacking passion, unadventurous, passive. The difference is that it has the advantage of being practically gratis and does not interfere with the working capacity. It also gives pleasure and helps people forget the worries and pains of their daily lives. (This would in fact be a disadvantage in a society where it is vital that people buy the maximum of what they can afford, provided that people buy fewer commodities because they are occupied with sexual consumption. But this is not so—in the first place, because sexual consumption stimulates the need for consumption in general and thus helps to produce the necessary level of greed. In the second place, although sexual intercourse as such does not require any expenditure of money (except to buy contraceptives), it does lead indirectly to more consumption in areas such as travel, cosmetics, apparel, and other commodities and services that are intended to enhance sexual attractiveness.) A consumer culture must insist, as it were, on sexual freedom, even if it does so through the remarkable feat of double-talk and a strict insulation between the official ideology and the sanctioned practice.

It has often been said that the sexual revolution was largely caused by Freud's work; but this conclusion confuses cause and effect. In the first place, Freud's was a Victorian pathos, and he never had any sympathy with sexual practices beyond those prescribed by the morals of his society. His defense of masturbation was about the boldest step he took with respect to freer sexual practices. Second, and more important, had it not been for the needs of a consumer culture, Freud would not have become so popular. The popularization of Freud's theories was a handy, semiscientific rationalization for the change in mores that would have happened anyway in the period after 1920.

Sexuality and the New Life-Style of the Hippie Movement

Sex as an article of consumption is a product of the second industrial revolution; its impact is, if anything, reactionary and in no way revolutionary either politically or personally. (The opposition to the new sexual mores came—and still does come—from the older lower and middle classes, whose members were not affluent enough to participate in the new consumer culture and hence resented it. But the fact that the opponents of the sexual revolution were politically reactionary does not mean that the promoters and participants in the new sex-consumption are revolutionary or progressive.) However, the consumer sector of the sexual liberation movement does not represent the whole. Aside from the majority patterned along the lines of the consumption personality, there is a minority that represents exactly the opposite. This minority, consisting largely of the hippies and a part of the radical wing of the youth, is made up of radical critics of the consumer culture, in terms of both their ideas and their practice of life. They protest against the reification of man against his transformation into a "consuming thing"; they resent the alienation, the lack of joy, the idolatric submission to things, behavior patterns, slogans, and synthetic personalities; and they are sensitive to the point of being allergic to the sham and double-talk that prevail in our culture. Most of all, they are hungry for life; they want to *be* and not to *have* and to *use*. Insofar as they are politically concerned, they want a culture in which life rules over death and men rule over things.

I forgo as being irrelevant in this context a critique of the sexual liberation movement, particularly for its failure to develop a life-style for those over thirty or for the reliance of these people on drugs, for their break with the very tradition of which they are an upshot, and for their inability to find or to aim at a synthesis between the neo-matriarchal, anarchistic experience of equality and disorder and the neo-patriarchal acceptance of rational authority, structure, and a minimum of organization. Furthermore, their passivity seems to mold many of them as consumers at a low level of material needs; and their destructive-necrophilous traits motivate some of them, if only a minority. However, in spite of all this, for many of them sexual pleasure is a joy and primarily part of their hunger for an affirmation of life. It is an expression of love of life, though perhaps not in terms of the individual love that is supposed to exist in married life. It is part of being, not of possessing; and by overcoming the traditional stigma of sex, it shows a lack of lasciviousness among its alienated practitioners in the world of conformity.

In order to understand the hippies (to whom I refer broadly as having adopted a similar style of life and philosophy, including those who at the same time have a radical political philosophy), one must understand the hippie movement as an original religious mass movement, perhaps the only significant one in our time. It is, of course, a nontheistic movement, although it is based on faith in love, in life, in equality, and in peace. It is in complete opposition to the ruling purpose-bound worship of the machine. It is based on shared enthusiasm and certain rituals. The ways of dressing and wearing hair represent not only a protest against middle-class respectability but also a common ritual by which the members of the new religion identify themselves. I believe the same holds true, to some extent, for drug taking. Through drugs the hippies reach out for spiritual experience in the "instant" manner and, in this respect, contribute to the consumer culture; but drug taking is also a common ritual that permits the members of the new religion to experience union and solidarity. The gatherings of between 300,000 and 400,000 enthusiasts in New York State and of 200,000 at the Isle of Wight in the summer of 1969 were impressive demonstrations of the strength of this movement. Not only the number of people who gathered to listen to their favorite artists but also the order, lack of aggressiveness, general helpfulness, and good mood under the most trying circumstances facilitated a new spirit so visible that even the conservative local villagers were impressed and became helpful and sympathetic. In terms of the religious quality of the movement, the happening was not so much a mass visit to a concert as a pilgrimage, with all the attendant qualities of shared intention, interest, and experience. Yet considering the hippies' own limitations and the power of the established idolatry, it seems to me doubtful that they will survive.

Sexuality and Psychoanalysis:
The Relevance of Wilhelm Reich

Having distinguished between the sexual revolution as part of the consumer culture on the one hand and as part of a revolution for life on the other, we can take up once more the question of its relation to psychoanalysis. Although the fact remains, as earlier noted, that Freud did not sympathize with loose sexual mores and would probably have been shocked by the suburbanites as well as by the hippies, he nevertheless had opened a door. His thesis was that man's passions, all his intense strivings aside from those for self-preservation, were of a sexual nature; that, in fact, man as a passionate being was a sexual being. To be sure, unless sexuality was curbed and repressed, there could be no civilization; but the stuff of human strivings, beyond those for survival, was made of libido. W. Reich reproached Freud for not opening the door wider. Freud did not consider the prospect of a radical sexual revolution, which was to occur later. The one psychoanalyst who really opened the door to sexual revolution was Reich himself.

In my opinion, Reich's most important contribution in this respect was his lack of satisfaction with Freud's concept of genital potency. Freud did not raise the question about the *quality* of sexual experience. If a man was able to perform the sexual act successfully, he was considered to be genitally potent;

and by *successfully* was meant the ability to have an erection and to continue the sexual act long enough to give his partner a chance for an orgasm. On the basis of this criterion most men are genitally potent, and those who were absolutely or relatively impotent can be considered sick. Thus the sexual act was evaluated (from the biological standpoint) in terms of serving reproduction, with an allowance made for the woman's enjoyment.

Reich, who was concerned with the whole body as being relaxed and free as opposed to cramped, went a decisive step beyond Freud. He took into account the quality of the orgastic experience, not just its effectiveness. Moreover, he looked upon the genital organs not as instruments, originally meant to produce children, but as parts of the body able (together with the whole body) to experience ecstatic joy and freedom. His concept of genital potency exploded the limitation of the unpleasure-pleasure principle and entailed instead the response of the nonrepressed, nondefensive personality, of the total life-affirming and life-enjoying, free human being.

Reich developed a concept of sexual freedom that probably comes as close as any theoretical concept to the experience of the revolutionary wing of the sexual liberation movement. It is only logical that among its members Reich seems to enjoy a high degree of popularity. Had he not lost himself (at least in my opinion) in rather fantastic theories about "orgon" and so on, in connection with which he eventually became a martyr for his teachings, he probably would have followed the line of thought that connects sexuality with the whole personality. He might also have become an even more influential teacher for the sexual revolutionaries. But he made the error of believing naively in the immediate political consequences of the attitude of the sexually liberated youth. He wrongly assumed that because the reactionary adhered to a strict sexual morality, the opposite attitude characterized the revolutionary. Specifically, he failed to foresee that the Nazis would not adhere to the conservative standards of sexual morality.

Yet the connection—between sexual happiness and total happiness, physical relaxation and de-repression, sexuality and character, inner activity and greed, being and having—has not lost any of its importance. There is an urgent need to go much further with the research into this connection.

THE SEXUAL PERVERSIONS AND THEIR EVALUATION

The History of the Evaluation of Sexual Perversions

Thus far I have dealt with only *one* aspect of the sexual liberation: the consequences of the Christian strictures on "normal" sexual intercourse insofar as it does not serve the purpose of procreation. But the same stricture also affects another form of sexual activity, the perversions, which by their very nature do not lead to procreation. In fact, sexual perversion is defined as a sexual activity to the exclusion of the "normal" act of intercourse. The sexual perversions include sadism and masochism, anal and especially coprophilic sexuality, exhibitionism, voyeurism, transvestitism, oral-genital practices (even masturbation was once looked upon as a perversion), and all forms of homosexuality. One used to speak of "perversions" as if they were replacing the "normal" sex act completely or, in the case of homosexuality, making it impossible. But the term *perversion* was often not used to describe sexual acts leading to genital intercourse.

In recent years, however, it has become commonplace to exclude homosexuality, oral contact with the genitals, voyeurism, and exhibitionism from the category of perversions. The traditional definition of perversion, inasmuch as it was based on nonprocreation, quite obviously was not useful for arriving at any distinctions between different kinds of perversions. It was based on an ideological and theological definition of what was "natural" and "unnatural," not on the nature of the different desires and practices. But with the weakening and disappearance of this theological and moral ideology, the reactions of people to perversions have changed. This is as obvious in the case of homosexuality as it is in the case of oral-genital practices, which are considered by a large part of the population to be perfectly normal; in fact, many psychiatrists and psychoanalysts actually suspect the presence of neurotic factors when a person shows a reaction of disgust or repulsion toward these practices. On the other hand, almost everybody would consider the extreme cases of necrophilia (a male's desire to have intercourse with the corpse of a woman) or coprophilia (the desire to put excrement into the mouth) to be disgusting and sick. But what about the "perversions" in between these two extremes, especially sadism or masochism? Are they pathological drives, too, like coprophilia (though much less severe)? Or do they fall within the range of healthy desires, which are considered to be "unnatural and wrong" only because traditional morality has made them so?

It is not easy to answer these questions. Certainly a reaction of disgust in many, or even most, people proves nothing in itself. Such a reaction can readily be explained, and in two ways. First, the disgust may follow from the repression of corresponding tendencies in oneself, as in the case of disgust toward excrement. (In this case, most people would not feel the same disgust toward their own feces that they feel toward those of others.) Second, the disgust can be produced by the power of the parents' suggestion, which causes the child to feel disgusted with his excrement.

Those who argue in favor of perversions of any kind may state: If a man has the desire to beat, hurt, or humiliate a woman and, in the act of doing so, finds the maximum of sexual excitement and satisfaction, who is to say that his desire is wrong? Is not every desire worthy of satisfaction simply because it exists? And is this not especially so in the case of sadistic satisfaction, which is sought after not by the majority but, at any rate, by a considerable number of people? Might not this minority be transformed into a majority, if the inhibitions and, hence, the repression of this desire were lifted?

Certainly in the case of sadism there remains a difficulty. If one were to insist that a desire deserves fulfillment only if no other person is damaged, the sadist would have to find himself a masochistic woman (or vice versa) who enjoys the mutual action (or would have to compensate the partner by money, as in the case of prostitutes). But this difficulty can be solved. Although statistics are not available, we can assume that masochism and sadism occur often enough within the general population that nobody would have to be forced to do what he or she does not want to do, and probably nobody would have to be paid for it either.

Quite clearly, we have arrived at a more general discussion here: namely, one that concerns the principle that a person's desires, needs, or cravings ought to be fulfilled, whatever they might be. The underlying assumption is that all needs are of equal rank and that freedom consists in man's right to fulfill his needs and to do as he pleases, so long as he does not harm anybody else. But in considering this point of view we come across a somewhat paradoxical situation. This was the point of view of many members of the privileged classes, often expressed not ideologically but only in terms of their actions, whether we think of the French upper class in the eighteenth century or the British upper class in the nineteenth century. Philosophically it was systematized in the nineteenth century (e.g., by J. Bentham) and elevated to a dogma with the increasing mass consumption of the mid-twentieth century.

The theory that the fulfillment of all desires is allowed, or even desirable, was applied explicitly to everything except sex; yet the more advanced social groups have understood the implicit message very well. Thus far there is nothing puzzling in this development; on the contrary, it is a logical outcome of the socioeconomic development that occurred in the transition from a hoarding to a consumer society. What *is* puzzling, however, is that the same principle applied to sex and the perversions has been announced as a revolutionary principle, as one in full contradiction to bourgeois life—a claim that has been made more or less explicitly by various representatives of radicalism.

We can start here with de Sade himself. This man, one of the most radical thinkers of the French Revolution, denounced family, property, and religion as the archevils of society and gave vent to his sadistic-masochistic fantasies in his novels. The question arises as to whether de Sade indulged in these fantasies *because* he was an avant-garde revolutionary. Or were they characteristic of de Sade, a member of the upper class? And was his revolutionary attitude a reaction *against* his sadomasochistic other self?

The latter is most likely, given that his actions revealed a most kind man who risked his own life by condemning capital punishment. The "pornographic" literature goes from de Sade through surrealism down to the contemporary avant-garde of radical writers such as J. Genet or the author of *The Story of O* (Réage 1972). To this group of radical writers H. Marcuse also belongs, despite the remarkable intellectual trapeze act he has performed in keeping his readers guessing as to what his position in these matters is. (In this connection, see my critique in Chapter IV.)

The Psychoanalytic Evaluation of Perversions

Marcuse and others assume that perversions are bodily connected with certain erogenous zones or are partial components of the sexual drive that are not qualitatively different from all other libidinous desires. They also assume that perversions have no particular content relevant to the total person, either characterologically or in terms of his existential aims, and hence believe that their practice should be completely free and unquestioned. In this view sadomasochism is completely separated from the personality as a whole and is a value-neutral matter of taste. If this is so, then indeed any questioning about these perversions would be nothing but a manifestation of the anti-pleasure attitude of bourgeois society.

But this is not so, because perversions are related to the person's character and to the "spiritual" answer he gives to his life.

Let us begin with the simpler of these two problems, the connection between perversion and character. Take sadism and masochism as an example. Experience has shown that the person for whom sadistic practices are most exciting sexually is also a "sadistic character." In other words, outside the sphere of sexual activity this person exhibits the qualities of sadism in his relationships to other people. (In Fromm 1936a and 1941a I have given a detailed clinical description of the sadomasochistic [authoritarian] character.) The sadistic character is characterized by the desire for absolute control over others and the wish to hurt them. (There is also the variant known as benevolent sadism, in which the control functions not to hurt but to keep a person as sadistic property by "helping" and "furthering" him.) Sadism is contrary to love and to respect; it deprives the "object" of his freedom. But the sadist, too, is unfree and incapable of independence. Characterological sadism can be conscious but is usually unconscious and rationalized, for instance, as justified revenge, performance of duty, or nationalistic or revolutionary hatred in the fight for the just cause. In instances of overt sadistic perversion, the intensity of characterological sadism may be somewhat reduced because of its direct satisfaction in the sexual act. Even if our observation is directed to the unconscious part of the character, however, there is no doubt that the sadistic perversion is rooted in a sadistic character structure. Thus, sexual sadistic desire and characterological sadism are two aspects of the same system.

The same holds true for genuine masochism—the desire to be completely controlled, to be clay in the partner's hand. The anal aspect of sadism, of which coprophilia is one manifestation, also has clinically well-known qualities. The anal character, according to the incontestable clinical findings of Freud and others, tends to be stingy, stubborn, and excessively clean, orderly, and punctual. Of secondary importance is the question as to whether one accepts the classic interpretation that these character traits are sublimations of or reaction-formations against the anal impulses; or whether one accepts the theory that I have formulated in *Man for Himself* that they are the expression of a negative self-isolating possessive relatedness to people and things (inasmuch as the anal sphere is one of the main symbols and manifestations of this orientation). In any case, the anal character tends to have these qualities. Moreover, the person with a coprophilous perversion will not only have some of the anal traits but, more important, will be inhibited in his capacity to love.

Considering the connection between sexuality and character, this question must be posed: Is the sadistic and anal character one of the variants of personality, which in themselves make no difference in terms of value and desirability? Or are anal sadistic traits, even if they are very well adapted to a certain type of society, pathological from the standpoint of the ideal of the fully developed, loving, independent, caring personality? The answer is obvious, if one shares the belief in these values as they were formulated in the humanistic tradition, from Buddha and the prophets to Spinoza.

The more complicated question arises as to whether such values could be seen in Freud's system. As a natural scientist Freud tended to avoid all explicit value judgments. But they came in through the backdoor in his evolutionary scheme. The normal and desirable development is the full development of the libido, from primary narcissism to object libido in terms of the capacity to be independent and capable of loving. For Freud, regression to or fixation on a pregenital level is both understandable (and hence not subject to indignation) and a failure of development (and hence pathological and undesirable). Freud's implicit value judgments are expressed in evolutionary terms and in reference to psychopathology. Regression to the earliest level of libido development represents the most pathological (i.e., "worst") stage; achievement of genital supremacy is healthy (i.e., good). Clinically, things are even simpler. A certain type of severe obsessive, in Freudian theory, is characterized by anal-sadistic regression, and his analysis is largely taken up with the task of helping him to progress from the anal-sadistic to the genital level. Or the anal-sadistic regression may manifest itself in other symptoms such as difficulties in working or sexual impotence, or in purely characterological symptoms such as rigidity or lack of spontaneity. In any case, the analyst will look at the anal-sadistic regression as a pathological phenomenon, regardless of whether it expresses itself in sexual perversions, in a symptom, or in a person's character. Of course, smaller amounts of anal-sadistic regression do not produce such symptoms and are not viewed as pathological in themselves; but this is the case because they are small, not because the anal-sadistic regression in itself is considered to be healthy or desirable.

The fact that Marcuse's new evaluation of the reactivation of the infantile stages is the very opposite of Freud's implicit value system does not, of course, indicate that he is wrong; this contradiction is worth mentioning only because it refers to one of the many points on which Marcuse's postulates are in sharp contradiction to those of Freud. On the whole, however, he seems to want to give the impression that his speculations developed from and grew out of Freud's system.

The Perverse Experience of Sadism and That of the Anal Character

More important than the comparison between Marcuse's speculations and Freud's theories is the type of *experience* that occurs in the sadomasochistic or coprophilous perversion. Assuming the ideal case of a sadistic man and a masochistic woman whose types of sadism or masochism, respectively, correspond to each other such that desire, consent, and satisfaction are mutual, the very nature of the sexual interrelation is one of unrelatedness in an affective sense. The two partners use each other for the satisfaction of their particular sexual desire, they exchange lust for lust, and they may even feel a certain mutual gratitude for the satisfaction they have received from each other. But in the very act of beating (or being beaten) each one remains fundamentally alone and the other remains an object. This is probably one of the reasons some men feel perfectly satisfied when they pay for the services of a prostitute, because they do not need to pretend any affectionate intimacy. But more than that, they do not even want affection, because the sadomasochistic desire by its very nature excludes it and makes it undesirable. The object of the sadist becomes a mere thing to him and he remains totally apart in his narcissistic self-involvement; the relationship is indeed inhuman if by that we mean another living being is transformed into a thing.

The difference between the storm trooper–prisoner situation and the "free libidinal relation" exists (Marcuse 1966, p. 203) but is only relative. Subjectively, the storm trooper's feelings toward his objects are qualitatively the same as those of the freely chosen partner—namely, feelings proceeding from the transformation of a living being into a thing.

The objection can be made that this mutual use of the other person as a mere *means* for the satisfaction of one's lust occurs also in the "normal" sexual act. This is true, of course, but there is a decisive difference as well. Although genital sexuality is not identical with a loving, affectionate attitude between two persons, it does at least permit it or, perhaps, furthers it. But the sadistic perversion, by its very nature, excludes love, intimacy, and respect.

The sadist sometimes feels affectionate after the act. This can be explained by his gratefulness for the received pleasure, or by the fact that his other self cannot stand the sadistic self and that he must prove to himself that he is human after all. By and large this postsadistic affection is often nothing but sentimentality (i.e., the alienation of real affection from the idea of what one ought or would want to feel); and, interestingly enough, it is not entirely rare among the most brutal "storm trooper" types, especially when they have been alone with their victims.

Both the sadistic sexual act and its underlying character substratum stand in contrast to love and respect. The kind of "pure" sadism of which Marcuse speaks is the denatured brainchild of psychoanalytic "philosophy" and lacks real existence. No more light is thrown on the phenomenon of sadism by Marcuse's statement that the term *perversion* covers "phenomena of essentially different origin"—namely, those instinctual manifestations that are "incompatible with repressive civilization, especially with monogamic genital supremacy" (Marcuse 1966, p. 203).

The very same point can—and must—be made with regard to other pregenital reactivations and perversions. Let us consider, for instance, the desires and interest based on anal libido. Is anal libido just another kind of excitement, with no reference to the total person and his character? Certainly not, according to Freud or to psychoanalysts who do not agree with the libido theory. One of the most fruitful discoveries in psychoanalysis was the finding that feces were represented in conscious feeling by dirt, money, and any possession. The *anal character* is deeply attracted by these equivalents of excrement and can be defined by this attraction.

In the simplest case the anal character loves possessions, money, property, and dirt. In fact, he tends to be possessive and dirty (the latter not so much in the physical as in the psychological sense). In more complicated cases, when cultural patterns or the person's values are inhospitable to the greed for money, or whatever, either this attraction is denied and a false front of opposite behavior patterns is adopted, or it is shown in areas where the discrepancy to the professed values is not easily visible (as in stinginess with feelings or words).

The reasons for this affinity between libidinous fixation and character have been proposed in several theories. The best known of these was offered by Freud and classic psychoanalysis. Freud assumed that the anal fixation is caused by particular experiences in childhood having to do with the function of elimination and the anal zone (cf. Freud 1908b, p. 169). Moreover, he viewed orderliness, parsimony, and obstinacy as direct sublimated outcomes of the anal erotic desires. Although this theory is neat and seems to be supported by the fact that stingy persons often exhibit a particular interest in and affinity with excrement, it has met with the objection that one finds many anal characters in whose childhoods no particular occurrences related to bowel training and so on can be observed. (The same objection exists with regard to the oral character, given that observation of humans as well as animal experiments have established that its development has little to do with the feeding process in infancy.)

In contrast to the description of the anal character as a by-product of anal repression, I have offered an explanation of the "hoarding character" (Fromm 1947a, pp. 65–67), which is based on the particular kind of relatedness of the person to the world outside. I shall not repeat it here in full. But I do give a brief account of my findings of anality in *The Heart of Man* (1964a, pp. 53–55). I have studied the meaning of feces and their attraction in terms of the experience of the person in the world. The feces are the product that is finally eliminated by the body, as they are of no further use to it. (That they are of use to the soil is another matter beyond the person's experience of his bodily existence.) The feces are a symbol of all that is not alive (dead) because they are not conducive to man's living process, insofar as he experiences it. They are perceived by the child, as Freud has demonstrated, as possession or property. And they are the first experience of having, in contrast to being, as experienced in the act of sucking, for instance. To take in food is a life-serving experience; and to get rid of excrement is a physiological necessity. In fact, a most distinct case of pleasure is nothing but the relief from unpleasureful tension; still, it is a matter of getting rid of something, not of taking in something. Of course, food intake and elimination, as objective facts, are equally necessary for life. But what matters psychologically is not the objective function but the subjective quality of the respective experience. The anal character is the one whose whole relatedness to the world is determined by the experience of having—and, more specifically, of having that which is dead. In its milder and, as it were, "benign" forms, the anal character is attracted by property and the wish to possess, whereas in its more intense and malignant forms he is attracted to decay, death, illness, destruction, and all else that is not alive but works against life. In the malignant form of the anal character, the necrophilous character, the desired aim is death and destruction. The difference between the anal and the necrophilous character seems to me mainly one of intensity of the death-loving, destructive forces. I have proposed that the necrophilous character be considered the malignant aspect of the anal character. The difference is essentially one of quantity and not of quality; hence the anal character is also thing and not life oriented, centered on having and not being.

The opposite of the necrophilous character is the biophilous, life-loving character, which roughly corresponds to Freud's "genital" character. (Freud never went beyond a rudimentary description of the genital character, however, in contrast to his rich description of the pregenital character orientations.) The (genital) life-oriented character and the (anal) thing or death-oriented character can be distinguished by certain general traits. The life-loving person, in contrast to the hoarding character, is attracted by the process of life and growth in all spheres. He prefers to construct rather than to retain. He is capable of wondering, and he prefers to see something new over the security of finding confirmation of the old. He loves the adventure of living more than he loves certainty. His approach to life is functional rather than mechanical. He sees the whole rather than only the parts, structures rather than summations. He wants to mold and to influence through love, reason, and his example; not by force, by cutting things apart, by the bureaucratic manner of administering people as if they were things. He enjoys life and all its manifestations more than mere excitement.

More specifically, the intensely anal (necrophilous) person can be recognized by his symptomatology, dreams, and behavior patterns, and often by his physical features and gestures as well. His skin looks dead, and in his gestures he marks the frontier between himself and the world outside of him. In the more extreme case, he wears a permanent smirk rather than a smile, and the expression on his face looks as if he were smelling a bad odor.

The foregoing description of anal character was necessary to convey, albeit sketchily, what anal regression and fixation mean both empirically and clinically. Again, as in the case of the sadistic perversion, what is meant by a different kind of "pure" anality, which will flower in the nonrepressive society, remains nebulous. If it is not characterized by the hoarding, nonloving, and nonsharing that constitute the most general qualities of anality in psychoanalytic terms, what is it beyond a mere figment of theoretical imagination separated from empirical data?

THE REVISION OF PERVERSIONS, USING SADISM AS AN EXAMPLE

Manifestations and the Essence of Sadism

Sadism, as I have said before, is not simply the wish to hurt or humiliate; it is the desire for absolute control over another being, whether human or animal. The wish to hurt and to humiliate is one of the most frequent manifestations of this wish; but complete power, even with a degree of benevolence, is a manifestation of sadism. In fact, the wish for control is often the only manifestation of the sadistic relationship to others; it is to be found in many bureaucrats, school teachers, nurses, parents (vis à vis their children), and so on. Often the sadism manifests itself only in this socially acceptable and easily rationalized attitude, either because more intense expressions of sadism are repressed and released only when socially approved (as in the "storm trooper" situation) or because the desire is not that intense and thus can be satisfied by some degree of control. There are many transitions between control and the infliction of pain.

Tying up, blocking, choking, and strangling another person, to suppress spontaneity and the expressions of his will, are such intermediate stages; they are intermediate not necessarily because they cause less suffering and pain than other forms of cruelty but because they are socially more acceptable and can easily be rationalized as intended in the interests of the "object." In these cases the sadist is usually entirely unconscious of the sadistic nature of his behavior, whereas in cases of overt cruelty the repression of this awareness is more difficult; yet there are many instances even of overt cruelty that are rationalized as necessary for the development of the child (as when a child is taught to "obey").

The sadistic desire is for complete, absolute control, at least over one object, or for a short moment. This wish is visible in the sexual relationship. For the male sadist, the woman must become pure object, his creature, a thing with which he can do as he likes without restrictions. (For the female sadist it is the same in reverse.) When sadism is combined with genital sexual desires, there follows a certain physiological satisfaction that limits the further extension of the sadistic action. If it is not combined with sex, the excitement is ended only when one's aim has been attained or when natural tiredness sets in. In the chronic forms of more hidden sadism, the desire is practically never satisfied.

Examples of sadism not directly linked to sexual desire and not combined with genital release include the cruelties of the storm troopers in concentration camps and in occupied territories, the beatings of prisoners or "suspects" by sadistic policemen, and the activities of lynch mobs. In such cases, helpless people, just because they are helpless, arouse the sadistic lust of the sadist and serve him as objects. Very frequent expressions of sadism can be seen in people's merciless beating of animals; the more benign form of sadism, that of control, is a motive often hidden in the "affection" that people have for pets— especially dogs, who lend themselves to be controlled or to be cowed (in contrast to cats).

A most illuminating manifestation of sadism is to be found in the "rape-rob" syndrome of soldiers in a conquered city. It is an old custom in warfare whereby soldiers who have conquered a city are given permission, explicitly or implicitly, to do with the inhabitants entirely as they please without any restrictions. This permission is usually restricted timewise; otherwise there might be the danger that some soldiers would do as they pleased within their own group and cease to obey their officers. We saw this behavioral syndrome in the "rape of Nanking" by Japanese troops and in the raping orgy of the Russian troops immediately after their conquest of Berlin. The peculiarity of the "rape-rob" syndrome is precisely that it is not confined to raping; the whole syndrome consists of raping, robbing, and destroying everything at hand, such as furniture, windows, and articles of use. Although killing also occurs, it is relatively rare and much less prominent. The soldiers engaged in these actions are uncontrolled and almost uncontrollable; they act with fierce passion, in a state of extremely intense excitement.

What is the meaning of this syndrome? The most obvious explanation would be to single out the raping as the central element and to interpret it as the result of a long-pent-up sexual drive that, after months or years of warfare, can be satisfied for the first time. Although it is of course true that prolonged sexual frustration is one element in this behavioral complex, several factors bring this explanation into question. First of all, in this syndrome the behavior toward women is characterized by its emphasis on rape, rather than by any even crude forms of persuasion and seduction. The obvious answer, that virtually all women would reject sexual advances in any case, is not, in my opinion, as convincing as it sounds; but in order to be sure, a study of this complex problem with reference to the data from various wars would be necessary. At any rate, the objection has some validity, but it does not adequately explain the phenomenon of the immediate and preferred use of rape. An example of the preference for rape when there was no problem about consent can be found in a study of a small Mexican village (cf. Fromm and Maccoby 1970b).

Another objection to the "sexual-frustration" explanation is the indiscriminateness of the choice. According to all reports, no woman was spared; old or unattractive women were raped indiscriminately. None of these reservations is in itself a compelling argument against the frustration theory. They gain in importance, however, if one considers the other aspects of the syndrome. The soldiers engaged in the aforementioned "rape-rob" orgy stole everything they could carry away, and what they could not steal they destroyed, dirtied, and stomped on. If they were motivated mainly by sexual lust, why would their robbing and destroying be acted out with equal intensity? And how do we explain this state of fierce excitement with its trance-like quality?

I have dwelled so long on the description of this syndrome because it is an excellent example of sadism. The core experience seems to be that of absolute and unrestricted power over everything and every person. By raping women, sadistic men establish absolute power over the living; not only the women themselves but also their parents, men, children, and friends are rendered powerless. Inasmuch as the woman represents for the man all of nature, in relationship to whom there is always an element of fear, unrestricted power over her goes with the sense of omnipotence that is the very essence of sadism. But this absolute power is experienced not only with regard to the living but also with regard to things. If one cannot make oneself into their master by carrying them away and using them, one can become their master by destroying them, or making them useless for others—by stamping them, as it were, with one's own ego.

This concept of sadism is principally different from that in which sadism is understood as a partial drive, essentially one of a sexual nature. It is something much more profound; it is a way of being, one of the possibilities of human existence, one of the answers that man can give to the question he is asked by being born human.

In what sense is sadism a "spiritual" answer to man's existential problem? The goal of all sadistic striving is control, absolute control, omnipotence. This is a solution unlike regression to animal existence and drug taking, which obliterate awareness and hence the source of the existential dichotomy. In the experience of omnipotence, another existential dichotomy is solved as well: Man explodes the limitations of his real existence as a human by obliterating the powerlessness inherent in this existence. Man, who has mind and fantasy, can imagine having power over everything and being "the master of his own ship"; but he cannot help experiencing, in reality, his powerlessness against many circumstances and eventually against death. This dichotomy between the vision of power and powerlessness can be resolved in the fantasy and practice of omnipotence. The sadist, who through various sadistic techniques achieves the experience of control, succeeds in transcending the human condition, in breaking down existential limitations. In the ecstasy of complete control, man ceases to be man; he is God. Maybe for a moment only, or an hour, or a day—but the hope for this experience and the experience itself are worth any other suffering, including even death. Only if one fails to grasp the "spiritual" meaning of sadism can one be satisfied dealing with it as a partial component of the sexual drive and as a psychological "aberration"; but in this way one will never understand its depth and intensity, nor its ubiquity.

The Social Determination of Sadism

Sadism differs according to whether the sadist has power or is powerless in reality. The average man is relatively powerless: the slave more than the serf, the serf more than the burgher, the worker of the nineteenth century more than the worker of the twentieth century, the member of a dictatorial police state more than the member of a democracy. Yet all are dependent on circumstances that are not of their doing and on persons not of their choosing (in a democracy, because they do not really "know" their representatives and may have "chosen" under the influence of intense brainwashing by television and other means of "communication"). To the degree that man has some power and can manifest his potency in meaningful acts, his feelings of powerlessness are reduced to a tolerable level; indeed, we find a good deal less sadism in the culturally and economically more advanced social classes than in the more backward classes, such as the lower middle class. (Cf. Fromm 1941a, pp. 207–239.)

The man who has little real material and cultural satisfaction in life, who is little more than the helpless object of higher powers, suffers intensely from his powerlessness: For him the sadistic solution of sadism is the only form of transcending his powerlessness; it is in fact the only form of personal liberation, unless he can participate in the constructive change of his circumstances, which, however, is made difficult by his sadism. But the impoverished human being who is and feels like Mr.

Nothing can become a king when, as a member of a lynch mob, he participates in the act of frightening, humiliating, and eventually killing his victim. And the equally poor member of a conquering army becomes God when, in the ecstasy of raping and robbing, he transcends his own social and human form of existence.

At the other end of the scale is the individual who in reality has such a degree of power that he is tempted to become God by transcending the human status. A political leader endowed with absolute power, such as Stalin or Hitler, is almost bound to fall into the temptation of absolute power. Camus brilliantly portrayed this phenomenon in his play *Caligula*. The office of absolute power gives Caligula the power over everybody—the bodies, the souls, the honor, the shame of everybody. Having this experience of unrestricted power, he cannot tolerate the existential powerlessness he still feels; in fact, in the exercise of his power he must destroy all human bonds and finds himself in a state of unbearable isolation. Only the fantasy of omnipotence, of being God, can save him from this pain. He is almost bound to attempt the impossible, "to want the moon." At this point he is insane. But this insanity is not a "sickness"; rather, it is a way of being, a private religion.

Sadism exists not only in the lower middle class and among dictators but also among many other social groups. In many private situations a person has the chance to play the role of dictator: There is the father in relation to wife and children, the school teacher, the prison guard, the policeman, the physician, the nurse, the army officer, and so on. It is important to note that in many of these instances the real power may not even be extreme; what matters is that the power is big enough to allow a person to have the fantasy of absolute power.

But since these situations at best facilitate the manifestation of sadism, the question remains as to whether its roots are in the individual who is not impoverished for socioeconomic reasons. Because the answer to this question would go beyond the scope of this chapter, I have to restrict myself to a general remark: The same conditions of factual powerlessness can be produced by the atmosphere of a family in which the growing child is exposed to sadistic treatment of the parents, especially in the less obvious forms whereby will and spontaneity are choked, either directly or by lack of any response, or by threats.

Sadism and Necrophilia

The problem of the connection between sadism and destructiveness is a most complicated one and still requires a great deal of investigation. (See my detailed discussion on this topic in *The Anatomy of Human Destructiveness,* 1973a.) We might have to distinguish between "simple sadism," the aim of which is to control and not to destroy, and destructive sadism, in which the possessive "anal" element has assumed the malignant form of attraction to death. This assumption corresponds to my concept of love of death (necrophilia) as the malignant form of the hoarding, "anal character," as I developed it in *The Heart of Man* (1964a, pp. 37–61). It goes without saying that, as with all mixtures, there are endless variations on the strength of the necrophilous factor.

In speaking about "simple" sadism, I must stress again that the aim of the sadist is to control and not to destroy. He wants his object alive, because only then can he feel the excitement and satisfaction of full control. If he destroys the object the experience of control is lost, because he cannot watch the humiliation and helplessness of his victim. Only exceptionally (though not rarely) does the "simple" sadist want to kill; he may wish to enjoy his victims' fright so fully that he is carried to the ultimate act of killing. From the sadistic standpoint, however, this would not be strictly necessary, as his wish for omnipotence may be such that the act of killing, of destroying the miraculous quality of aliveness in another, is the ultimate manifestation of his omnipotence. For this reason it is not always easy to distinguish clinically between sadism and destructiveness (necrophilia). But the difference exists nevertheless.

The destructive, necrophilous person primarily hates life and wants to destroy it, not to control. Whereas sadism is "hot," necrophilia is cold and detached. The sadist is still on the side of life, seeking for an ultimate satisfaction that he cannot get in any other way. But the destructive person has left the world of the living, as it were. In his despair about his own unaliveness there is no solace left but the satisfaction that he can take life; hence, whereas simple sadism is a perversion of potency, destructiveness is the final and violent revenge on life for one's inability to experience any "intimacy," not even that between torturer and his victim.

Destructive sadism, in contrast to "simple" sadism, is characterized by the admixture of necrophilous tendencies; there is both the craving for omnipotence and the love of death. Given the presence of both tendencies, destructive sadism differs from simple sadism inasmuch as destruction of life is mixed with the craving for omnipotence; but it also differs from necrophilia in that the latter lacks the "hot" relationship to the victim. A lynch mob is one of the best examples of destructive sadism; a certain type of cold-blooded murder (without sadistic elements) exemplifies necrophilous destructiveness; and the desire to hurt and humiliate without killing is an example of "simple" sadism.

In his theory of the death instinct, Freud offered a much more attractive solution by suggesting that sadism and Eros are blended with the death instinct. But this solution is not satisfactory either—first, because it does not explain nonsexual sadism, and, second, because at best it would be useful to

109

explain destructive sadism but not simple sadism. Its main shortcoming, however, is the lack of distinction between control-omnipotence and destruction-necrophilia.

On the basis of clinical as well as social-psychological data, I have come to the conclusion that sadism is a form of intense personal relatedness in which the sadist needs to become the ruler over another person in order to be whole. In short, sadism involves a "symbiotic" relationship. The sadist wants and needs the other person passionately but not lovingly, as we use the term in its usual sense. He is greedily attached to the other person in his own sadistic way. And it is for this reason that sadism, like other forms of intense attachment, easily incites and blends with genital sexuality.

4

The Alleged Radicalism of Herbert Marcuse

I feel it is necessary to deal specifically with the writings of H. Marcuse for two reasons: First, his position is exactly opposite the one presented in my books, although in some respects there are affinities to the line of critical thought that I expressed not only in my early writings at the beginning of the 1930s but also in *Escape from Freedom* (1941a) and in subsequent books. I believe it might clarify the position of the present book if I discuss, albeit briefly, some of the main theories developed by Marcuse.

The second and more important reason is that Marcuse, because of his misinterpretation of Freud and Marx as well as his often confused and contradictory thought, tends to confuse many readers, especially the radical left. I believe that this effect is dangerous. If radical thought ceases to be critical and rational, it ceases to be "radical" (in the sense of "going to the roots") and becomes adventurist or leads to irrational actions. Furthermore, the new left, like most of the young generation today, is not very well acquainted with the literature of the past and, in becoming familiar with a distorted Freud and a distorted Marx, will be of no help in making a connection with the humanist and revolutionary tradition.

MARCUSE'S UNDERSTANDING OF FREUD

I hesitate to accuse an intelligent and erudite man like Marcuse, who has written one brilliant and profound book, *Reason and Revolution* (1941), of the misinterpretation of the works he discusses. As I am sure he does not distort willfully and intentionally, there must be powerful personal motives that make him unaware of the absurdity of what he writes in *Eros and Civilization* (1955/1966) and *One-Dimensional Man* (1964). Whatever they are, I shall stick strictly to the argument he presents and attempt to answer it in the following pages.

Before launching into my criticism of his presentation of Freud's theories, I must point to one weakness that Marcuse himself mentions without being sufficiently aware of its implication. He claims that he is dealing only with Freud's theories and that he is neither familiar with nor competent in the clinical application of psychoanalytic findings. This "philosophy" of psychoanalysis, which is unrelated to clinical knowledge, is an approach that greatly handicaps the understanding of psychoanalytic theory. When taken out of their clinical context, Freud's findings become abstract theories; and thus it becomes impossible to evaluate the real meaning of Freud's theories, which is rooted in his clinical observation.

Marcuse's basic misinterpretation of Freud's position lies in his attempt to interpret Freud as a revolutionary thinker. Freud was a typical representative of nineteenth-century bourgeois, mechanistic materialism and an optimistic liberal reformer until World War I; but he despaired of all social change for the better from then on. In *Civilization and Its Discontents* (1930a), he expressed his negative attitude toward socialist or revolutionary aims with unmistakable clarity. But the roots for this attitude can be found in his earlier work. He assumed that civilization is based on the repression of the libidinous instinct and that it results from a sublimation or reaction formation, for which this repression was a condition. Accordingly, he believed, man is confronted with the following alternative: Either no repression and hence no civilization; or repression and hence civilization but, in many cases, also neuroses.

Freud's sympathies were undoubtedly on the side of civilization and repression. But, like many liberal reformers, Freud thought that sexual repression went too far, and that if repression were decreased, neuroses could also be decreased without endangering the basic structure of society. He also believed firmly in the necessary conflict between instinctual needs and civilization, and had no doubts about the validity and necessity of the existing form of bourgeois society. Thus he was opposed to socialism—an opposition that constituted one main element in his hostility against W. Reich, who tried to combine his communist ideas (to which he adhered at the time of his conflict with Freud but which he denounced later on) with a radical theory about sexual liberation.

It seems astounding that the liberal antisocialist Freud should be transformed into a revolutionary. Sometimes Marcuse distinguishes between the Freud whom he supports and certain statements by Freud that he criticizes. As a result, discussion of this topic is somewhat difficult. Indeed, Marcuse's argumentation is slippery. He makes proper qualifications of his approval of Freud but on the whole gives Freud the role of a revolutionary thinker.

How is this possible? As far as I can see, one answer is that Marcuse is impressed by Freud's "materialism." Marcuse considers the instincts to be the real and material needs of man, and everything else is rationalization or ideology. This answer could be satisfactory if we were dealing with an author who is less aware than Marcuse of the difference between mechanistic materialism and Marx's "historical materialism." Marcuse specifically expressed opposition to the former.

In the beginning of *One-Dimensional Man* (1964), Marcuse seems to put all his hope in the perfection of the technological process.

> The technological processes of mechanization and standardization might release individual energy into a yet uncharted realm of freedom beyond necessity. The very structure of human existence would be altered; the individual would be liberated from the work world's imposing upon him alien needs and alien possibilities. The individual would be free to exert autonomy over a life that would be his own. If the productive apparatus could be organized and directed toward the satisfaction of the vital needs, its control might well be centralized; such control would not prevent individual autonomy, but render it possible. (Marcuse 1964, p. 2)

What is this "yet uncharted realm of freedom beyond necessity"? Marcuse is extremely vague in describing what he really means. In *Eros and Civilization,* he mentions among the aims of the good society that men "can die without anxiety" and without pain and not earlier than "they must and want to die" (Marcuse 1966, p. 235). But it is hard to take these statements seriously because, in the first place (for psychological reasons that are related not to the social order but rather to heredity and constitution), there will always be men who die before they want to die. The demand that man die with a minimum of pain also rings hollow in a civilization where medical art does everything it can to alleviate the pain experienced in the process of dying. And as for the idea that a man has the right to take his life when he decides to do so, there are many today who agree with Marcuse; moreover, there is certainly no need for a fundamental change in society that would bring about better facilities for voluntary ending of life. Our suicide rate shows that, even under the present circumstances, nobody is seriously hindered from taking his life if he intends to do so.

Why elimination of the fear of death should play such an eminent role in Marcuse's ideal of the new man becomes clearer if one examines that ideal. It can be expressed very briefly if one cuts through the intellectual embellishments with which Marcuse somewhat beclouds the issue. If man in the completed technological society no longer has to worry about work because all his material needs are fulfilled, then he can regress to becoming a child again or, perhaps, an infant. Marcuse does not say this in so many words because it would sound too absurd or daring if spelled out. Nevertheless he makes this ideal sufficiently clear if one follows his reasoning in detail.

One manifestation of the new infant-life existence is what Marcuse calls polymorphous sexuality. What does this mean? In Freudian theory it is the sexual experience of the child before puberty, especially before the blossoming of the Oedipus complex, at around age 6. During this period the whole body is libidinized and not only the genitals but all erogenous zones (particularly the rectum and the mouth, but also other aspects of pregenital sexuality such as sadism and masochism) are sources of sexual enjoyment. Then, with the awakening of phallic sexuality and finally genital sexuality around puberty, pregenital sexual pleasure becomes subordinated to genital sexuality.

Marcuse's idea is that this subordination of pregenital to genital sexuality is characteristic of all repressive societies, and that in a free society pregenital sexuality will come into its own again and lose the characteristics that we attribute today to "perversions." The essential point of this theory is that man, in order to become fully himself, must regress to being a child again—a regression that must be expressed in the new flowering of pregenital sexuality. But, or so Marcuse's theory goes, in a nonrepressive society such manifestations of pregenital sexuality as coprophilia (love for feces) and sadism take on a meaning entirely different from the meaning such manifestations have in the repressive society. And when man regresses to childhood, all erogenous zones will be reactivated, resulting in "a resurgence of pre-genital polymorphous sexuality and . . . a decline of genital supremacy" (Marcuse 1955/1966, p. 201). If the body in its entirety becomes "an instrument of pleasure . . . a change in the form and scope of libidinal relations would lead to a disintegration of the institutions in which the private interpersonal relations have been organized, particularly the monogamic and patriarchal family" (1955/1966, p. 201). For Marcuse, liberation from exploitation and irrational authority is paralleled by the liberation of sexuality "constrained under genital supremacy to the erotization of the entire personality" (1955/1966, p. 201).

THE CONCEPT OF PERVERSIONS

Marcuse states that perversions such as sadism have varying qualities, depending on the type of society in which they occur:

> The function of sadism is not the same in a free libidinal relation and in the activities of the S.S. Troops. The inhuman, compulsive, coercive, and destructive forms of these perversions seem to be linked with the general perversions of the human existence in a repressive culture, but the perversions have an instinctual substance distinct from these forms; and this substance may well

express itself in other forms compatible with normality in high civilization. (Marcuse 1955/1966, p. 203)

And when talking about his goal for the "new man" in a nonrepressive society—namely, the realization of infantile, pregenital sexuality—Marcuse states that "the libido would not simply reactivate precivilized and infantile stages, but would also transform the perverted content of those stages."

I find it impossible to understand what Marcuse is really talking about. After rereading these passages many times, I have even begun to doubt whether Marcuse had any clear idea of what he meant. To begin with, the fact that the sadism of a storm trooper is different from the sadistic behavior involved in the sexual interaction of two people, both of whom feel pleasure, is obvious. In the latter case the sadistic hurting or degrading of the sexual object is based on common consent; and even the humiliating practices characteristic of the sadistic perversion lack the seriousness and inhumanity of the sadist who uses his object by force. But though this difference exists and is important, it does not basically alter the content of the sadistic impulse: The desire for complete control over a human being, which deprives that human being of will, makes him or her a powerless object and manifests itself in the desire to hurt and humiliate the object.

Indeed, there is no greater manifestation of power than forcing a living being to endure pain. This content is not basically different from that involved in the practice of the sadomasochistic perversion, which is frequently found in our society and many others. If sadism does not have this aim—an aim that gives it its character and is the basis for the intensity of excitement and satisfaction, it is no longer sadism; but Marcuse fails to say *what* it is.

Of course, he does not speak of the sado-perversion in our "repressive" society (although the difference between storm troopers and the mutual voluntary sadism of a sadomasochistic couple still pertains today; but what remains of the content of sadism in the nonrepressive society? What does Marcuse mean when he says that the libido would not *simply* reactivate precivilized stages but *also* transform the perverted content? What is the perverted content of sadism, and what is it transformed into? What is the "instinctual substance" that, today, is distinct from the destructive forms of the perversion? Is the purified sadism not (or not *only*) sexual? Is the instinctual substance no longer characterized by the need to control, hurt, humiliate? And, if not, what is sadistic about it?

One would hope that the answer to these questions could be found in Marcuse's general statements about the regression to the infantile libido, which is supposed to be basically different from regression in the nonrepressive society. But, unfortunately, Marcuse's main thesis about the transformation of sexuality into Eros is equally vague; it jumps out of the head of this philosopher of psychoanalysis who misinterprets the meaning of Freud's concept, part of which he clearly misunderstands. This is not the place to discuss in detail Marcuse's misinterpretation of Freud. Interesting in this context, however, is the fact that Marcuse considers the reactivation of pregenital sexuality—that is, of the perversions—to be a desirable goal for human development, but he seems to be afraid to speak overtly in favor of the perversions; he wants them pure (there should be nothing ugly in the sadistic perversion) and, in order to describe this new and innocent "polymorphous sexuality," he postulates a metapsychological theory, changing and distorting Freud rather than discussing the clinical, experiential facts of sadism. He theorizes about perversions, narcissism, and so on, without ever trying to *describe* the phenomena. (Reflecting the abstract and unreal character of his "sadism" is the fact that he hardly ever speaks of masochism, which is inextricably connected with sadism and a necessary characteristic of the consenting partner of the sadist.)

It is a pity that Marcuse does not discuss another perversion, coprophilia, though he mentions it in passing. Coprophilia is the desire to touch, smell, and taste one's own or another's feces. According to Freud, it is a characteristic desire of infants during the phase dominated by the anus as erogenous zone. But it is not a rare perversion among adults today. Although it occurs far less frequently than the sadomasochistic perversion, it is often connected with strong sadism—hence the references to "anal-sadistic" character in psychoanalytic literature. According to Marcuse's general principle, this component of infantile sexuality should also be reactivated in the nonrepressive society.

But how is coprophilia "purified" while at the same time remaining coprophilia? The classic Freudian answer is that it becomes sublimated, as, for instance, in the pleasure taken in painting (in itself a rather questionable hypothesis). But given that Marcuse rejects sublimation, how is the interest and pleasure in feces expressed by the new and truly happy man? This question and the previous ones are so obvious that we can only conclude that Marcuse's praise of the perversions and of pregenital sexuality is softened by an idealizing tendency, a new Victorian prudishness phrased in terms of metapsychological theories.

The same critique holds true for one other infantile striving that Marcuse claims should be reactivated in the nonrepressive society: *narcissism*. Marcuse writes that the reactivation "of polymorphous and narcissistic sexuality ceases to be a threat to culture and can itself lead to culture-building if the organism exists not as an instrument of alienated labor but as a subject of self-realization—in other words, if socially useful work is at the same time the transparent satisfaction of an individual need" (1955/1966, p. 210). Yet although words like *self-realization* and *transparent* sound nice, it is hard to figure out what the new regression to narcissism is supposed to be, provided the term has a meaning that is even vaguely related to its psychological definition.

Marcuse does not make it easy to understand what he means in this respect. He offers his own interpretation of Narcissus, and his use of the term *narcissistic* does not correspond to the meaning given in Freud's theory (1955/1966, p. 162). This is clear and correct. But a few pages later, Marcuse attempts to proceed in the opposite direction and suggests that he may be able to "find some support for our interpretation in Freud's concept of primary narcissism" (1955/1966, p. 167). This is somewhat surprising inasmuch as Marcuse's own interpretation is that Narcissus "does not love only himself." Furthermore, if he is the antagonist of Eros and "if his erotic attitude is akin to death and brings death, then rest and sleep and death are not painfully separated and distinguished" (1955/1966, p. 167). Regardless of the validity and meaning of this interpretation, it is in precise opposition to Freud's concept of narcissism, in which the narcissist loves only himself; and, of course, in opposition also to Freud's later theory whereby narcissism belongs to Eros and hence does not possess the affinity to death that Marcuse describes. Marcuse tries to save his claim by pointing to Freud's concept of primary narcissism. He also quotes Freud's statement about the "oceanic feeling," an essentially mystical experience that Freud explains is experienced as a regression to the earliest state of development, before any sense of individuality or self has yet developed. Again, as in previous instances, Marcuse uses Freud's terms, but either gives them a new meaning or takes away from them their specific and experiential meaning.

The Alleged Radicalism of Herbert Marcuse

It has become customary today, among those who claim to understand Freud's teachings, to emphasize Freud's libido theory rather than his theory of character. In doing so they throw overboard—or, rather, fail to take aboard—that part of Freud's theory without which the whole cannot be properly understood; they also remove the theory far enough from observable personal data that they are "protected" against the risk of ever coming to grips with their own character, particularly its unconscious aspects. Thus Freud becomes reduced to the liberator of sexuality and silenced as the pathfinder into the individual unconscious. Considering the discrepancy between the real Freud and the philosophically "interpreted" Freud, a psychoanalyst can hardly help assuming that the main reason for the distortion lies in the "resistance" against touching those central human problems consisting of the unconscious aspects of one's character and the results of one's repressions. This form of resistance has been greatly facilitated by the method that Marcuse and others have applied; in the first place, they deal only with Freud's metapsychology, not with his clinical findings; second, they largely ignore Freud's work before 1920 and concentrate mainly on his hypothesis of Eros and the death instinct (and this is essentially a metapsychological hypothesis, little related to clinical facts). Pieces of Freud's earlier hypothesis are brought into the picture, when these pieces fit the new philosophy of psychoanalysis; but the full knowledge and hence understanding of Freud's clinical data and the theories he built upon them are lacking. To simply state, as Marcuse does, that one is not concerned with clinical problems, and to consider them technical problems, is a methodological error given the nature of Freud's theories, which grew from the soil of empirical observation. It is about the same as discussing Marx's economic theories and claiming that no knowledge of economic reality is

121

necessary to understand Marx and to modify his theories in radical ways.

I cannot go into the many brilliant though evasive arguments that Marcuse uses to avoid shocking his reader—to avoid making him aware, perhaps, of what the ideal of the new man really amounts to. He is indeed faced with a formidable difficulty. To most people, the primacy of genital sexuality over sadistic, coprophilous, or other pregenital desire is not precisely the present from which they want to escape. In fact, they seem to find great happiness in genital fulfillment, especially when it is linked with personal love and intimacy.

In order to assuage the reactions of more normally oriented people, Marcuse uses two arguments. First, he states that

> the free development of transformed libido within transformed institutions, while eroticizing previously tabooed zones, time and relations, would *minimize* the manifestations of *mere* sexuality by integrating them into a far larger order, including the order of work. In this context, sexuality tends to its own sublimation: the libido would not simply reactivate precivilized and infantile stages, but would also transform the perverted content of these stages. (1955/1966, p. 202)

It is difficult to imagine the sexual reality to which Marcuse refers in this statement. Coprophilia, for instance, would be revived—that is, people would retain a pleasure in smelling, seeing, and tasting feces—but it would not be merely sexual (in the pregenital sense); rather, it would be integrated into the order of work. The same, I assume, holds true for sadism. Does this mean that a man who finds lustful enjoyment in beating or humiliating a woman does so only partly or not merely as a sexual pleasure, and that part of this pregenital pleasure is expressed in his work or by the larger social order? As far as the latter is concerned, Marcuse only repeats Freud, who assumed that pregenital sexuality is sublimated in culture (the famous example is the surgeon who has sublimated his sadism into the art of surgery). This sublimation of pregenital sexuality, therefore, does not constitute anything that has not happened in the repressed society. The new aspect of sublimation that Marcuse offers as the aim of the new man is the fact that pregenital sexuality is also experienced as sexual enjoyment in a relationship between one person and another.

A second way in which Marcuse tries to embellish the new idealization of perversions is to say that where sexuality is *suppressed* the libido "manifests itself in the hideous forms so well known in the history of civilization; in the sadistic and masochistic orgies of desperate masses, of society elites, of starved bands of mercenaries, of prison and concentration camp guards" (1955/1966, p. 202). The fact is that perversions such as coprophilia, sadism, and masochism have been widespread throughout history, and it depends to a large extent on the particular class and its social taboos as to whether they were practiced only with the assistance of prostitutes or in "free libidinal relations." (It seems that, at present, the middle and upper classes do very well in this respect without prostitution.) At any rate, a revolution is hardly necessary to bring about a flowering of perversions—if this were the desirable goal.

Certainly not, according to Freud. And Marcuse would have been more straightforward if he had stressed that his proposals for the revival of polymorphous sexuality were in strict contradiction to the whole of Freud's systematic thinking. In this respect Reich rightfully claimed that he was developing Freud's theory to its ultimate conclusions by emphasizing the overall importance of orgastic potency, as against the inhibiting elements to be found in the majority of people. Reich was referring, of course, to the liberation of genital sexuality from inhibitions, and not to the revival of pregenital sexuality and of perversions. He believed that if genital sexuality could be liberated, the increasing vital energy and freedom would lead to politically revolutionary attitudes. Although this point is debatable, it can certainly be argued; but that can hardly be said about Marcuse's connection between freedom from oppression and the primacy of genital sexuality.

But quite aside from the fact that, on this point, Marcuse uses Freudian theory to prove an ideal that is exactly the opposite of Freud's theory, there is the entirely different question of the psychological meaning of various perversions. It is a clinical fact that people who are attracted to feces, dirt, and so forth, tend not to love life, and that their relationships to other people are primarily sadistic. If all that matters is the subjective feeling of excitement, then, of course, the satisfaction of coprophilia or sadism is as good as the satisfaction of genital sexual intimacy and love. But if one's concept of human existence and joy transcends that of pleasureful, sensuous excitement, whatever its source may be, and if one believes that such human experiences as love, tenderness, and compassion are superior to sadism and the attraction to death and dirt, then indeed the revival of perversions, even with all of Marcuse's nice embellishments and qualifications, is a step backward from progressive human development. Marcuse's point of view is a sybaritic one whereby pleasureful excitement per se is the aim in life, hate is as good as love, and sadism is as good as tenderness; all that matters is physical thrill. I assume that here lies the reason why Marcuse speaks with such scorn about people who talk of love, concern, and responsibility in the present stage of society.

Another aspect of the ideal of total regression is Marcuse's interpretation of the Oedipus complex—that the "sexual craving" for the mother-woman is "the eternal infantile desire for the archetype of freedom: freedom from want" (1955/1966, pp. 269–270). In the fight against the separation from mother, Eros wages "its first battle against everything that the Reality Principle stands for: against the father, against domination, sublimation, resignation" (1955/1966, p. 270).

Marcuse does not even discuss such phenomena as love, tenderness, and narcissism because, according to him, a sane man in our society cannot experience any of these phenomena and would only have the choice between declaring himself insane or admitting that all these experiences are for him nothing but ideologies. He uses a peculiar distortion of the Freudian theory to make all this appear as if it were the result of, or at least compatible with, Freud's thinking. But he can do that only by distorting Freud considerably. Freud's basic assumption was that man in any given society would have to cease being an infant and arrive at an optimum of independence. Freud's ideal was the mature, rational, independent man who could rely on himself and his own reason. Nobody would be more shocked than he to serve as the basis for the ideal of regression as the real aim of human progress. If Marcuse had been capable of examining the problem of the new man in his relationship to others, he might have discovered that sadism, masochism, voyeurism, exhibitionism, and narcissism—all of which are characteristic of infantile experience—would disturb any form of social cooperation in the "free society."

THE IDEALIZATION OF HOPELESSNESS

Another important point to be noted is the revolutionary role of those values which, according to Marcuse, have lost their validity: love, the wish for freedom, the fight against boredom and manipulation, and the desire for integrity and for life beyond material and sensuous satisfaction. To the extent that man has developed historically beyond the sphere of sheer satisfaction of his material needs, he has attained these "humane" experiences; and they have motivated him to fight against the many social orders that have violated these human demands and needs. Indeed, revolutions result not only from material deprivation but also from the lack of fulfillment of those human wishes without which we would not be fully human.

Herbert Marcuse makes short shrift of this problem. And in his polemic against my position he claims that the goal of optimal development of an individual's personality is "essentially unattainable" (1955/1966, p. 258) in our society; that one cannot practice "the productive realization of the personality, of care, of responsibility and respect for one's fellow men, of productive love and happiness and still remain sane"; and that "it would mean 'curing' the patient to become a rebel or (which is saying the same thing) a martyr" (1955/1966, p. 258).

Marcuse implies that I believe this aim is easy to achieve and can be achieved by the majority; however, he fails to acknowledge that throughout my work I have taken the unequivocal position that it is in full contradiction to the goal and practices of capitalist society. In *The Art of Loving* (1956a, p. 132) I wrote that

> I do not wish to imply that we can expect the present social system to continue indefinitely, and at the same time to hope for the realization of the ideal of love for one's brother. People capable of love under the present system are necessarily exceptions; love is by necessity a marginal phenomenon in present-day Western society. . . . Those who are seriously concerned with love as the only rational answer to the problem of human existence must, then, arrive at the conclusion that important and radical changes in our social structure are necessary, if love is to

become a social and not a highly individualistic marginal phenomenon.

But quite aside from the polemic involving me, what does Marcuse mean? That it is impossible for anyone, even a minority, to respect, care, and love? If this were so, it would seem to follow that one should not care, respect, and love; that one should not develop as a person but, instead, should wait for the revolution, when the "new man" will be born.

If it were not possible today to transcend the dominant personality pattern, it would never have been possible, and human progress could hardly have occurred. With such a conviction as that held by Marcuse, people in every age would have waited for revolution before trying to achieve a higher level of human development; and the revolution would have failed totally in its human goals (and not only partially, as was mostly the case) because it was made exclusively by people who had remained slaves.

The development of personality can and does take place in the most adverse circumstances; in fact, it is stimulated by their very existence. But this holds true only for a minority who, for a number of reasons, can free themselves to some extent from the social mode of thought and experience, and react against it. Marcuse and those who think like him do not for a moment deny this in the case of the radical, who can think what is generally "unthinkable" in his society. As for the attempt to achieve some of the experience of the "new man" "prematurely," as it were, it is difficult but not impossible. And it must be tried precisely by those who are opposed to present-day society and are fighting for a world fit for man to live in. Political radicalism without genuine human radicalism will only lead to disaster.

What Marcuse advocates in his sophisticated but ambiguous way is basically a vulgar materialism in which the complete satisfaction of material needs plus the satisfaction of all libidinal needs, especially the pregenital ones, constitute the final happiness.

It is not surprising that with this attitude one can only be hopeless and rather unhappy. And it is unfortunate that this hopelessness is translated into a political theory that lacks any sense of reality: "The outcasts and outsiders, the exploited and persecuted of other races and other colors, the unemployed and the unemployable" (Marcuse 1964, p. 256), although their consciousness is not revolutionary, have a revolutionary function. "The fact that they start refusing to play the game may be the fact which marks the beginning of the end of a period" (1964, p. 257). And Marcuse speaks vaguely about the chance that "the historical extremes may meet again: the most advanced consciousness of humanity, and its most exploited force. It is nothing but a chance" (1964, p. 257).

Marcuse ends *One-Dimensional Man* with the statement: "The critical theory of society possesses no concepts which could bridge the gap between the present and its future" (1964, p. 257). Any theory that possesses no concepts that could bridge the gap between the present and its future is for this very reason not applicable to political action. For political action of any kind demands demonstration of the ways and means by which the gap between present and future is bridged. Marcuse himself does not claim any political program; nor has he disclaimed any political actions, especially among students who believe that he has given a program for political action. He takes the proud position of "holding no promise and showing no success; it [this position] remains negative. Thus it wants to remain loyal to those who, without hope, have given and give their life to the Great Refusal" (1964, p. 257).

I am afraid that this introduction of romantic martyrdom into a position that has nothing to offer politically or humanly to help people in their next step toward the future—or, if there is none, to tolerate the catastrophe with dignity—may be appealing to some similarly minded people who dwell in despair. It is certainly an attitude that is not in line with the tradition of all those who have lived for and, if necessary, given their lives for those human values which, in Marcuse's thinking, have been discarded. On hopelessness and fear one can hardly build any political action, but one can do a good deal of damage by persuading others that the most progressive and radical theory has no better advice to give than to be proud of one's hopelessness.

Marcuse's pose as a radical who practices the Great Refusal, when he basically proposes a return to a childish sybaritic and egotistical experience, is a bitter joke. He does not speak in the name of life; he speaks in the name of the absence of love of life and of cynicism masquerading as a super-radical theory.

Since writing the above lines I have read Marcuse's recently published *An Essay on Liberation* (1969), in which he presents views that are in sharp contrast to his previous writings. Here the power of the death instinct seems to have been reduced almost to nothing, the reactivation of pregenital sexuality and the perversions has been dropped, and Marcuse now suggests that those who fight for socialism must anticipate in their own lives the qualities of the desired goal: "Exploitation must disappear from the work and general relations among the fighters. . . . Understanding, tenderness toward each other, the instinctual consciousness of that which is evil . . . would . . . testify to the authenticity of the rebellion" (1969, p. 88). Although I am glad that Marcuse has adopted a position that is essentially the one he criticized so sharply before, it is regrettable that he does not even comment on this change in the interests of intellectual clarity.

Bibliography

Bowlby, J., 1958: "The Nature of the Child's Tie to the Mother." *International Journal of Psychoanalysis,* Vol. 34.

Christiansen, B., 1963: *Thus Speaks the Body: Attempts Toward a Personology from the Point of View of Respiration and Postures* (Oslo: Institute for Social Research).

Eckhart, M., 1956: *Meister Eckhart,* selected by J. M. Clark (Edinburgh: Nelson and Sons).

Fenichel, O., 1953: "A Critique of the Death Instinct," in *The Collected Papers of Otto Fenichel,* First Series, collected and edited by H. Fenichel and D. Rapaport (New York: W. W. Norton, 1953), pp. 363–372.

Freud, S., 1953–1974: *The Standard Edition of the Complete Psychological Works of Sigmund Freud,* Standard Edition, (S.E.), Vols. 1–24 (London: Hogarth Press).

———, 1908b: *Character and Anal Eroticism,* S.E., Vol. 9, pp. 167–175.

———, 1912–1913: *Totem and Tabu,* S.E., Vol. 13.

———, 1920g: *Beyond the Pleasure Principle,* S.E., Vol. 18, pp. 1–64.

———, 1921c: *Group Psychology and the Analysis of the Ego,* S.E., Vol. 18, pp. 65–143.

———, 1923b: *The Ego and the Id,* S.E., Vol. 19, pp. 1–66.

———, 1927c: *The Future of an Illusion,* S.E., Vol. 21, pp. 1–56.

———, 1930a: *Civilization and Its Discontent,* S.E., Vol. 21, pp. 57–145.

———, 1931b: *Female Sexuality,* S.E., Vol. 21, pp. 221–243.

———, 1933a: *New Introductory Lectures,* S.E., Vol. 22, pp. 1–182.

———, 1933b: *Why War?* S.E., Vol. 22, pp. 195–215.

131

Bibliography

————, 1940a: *An Outline of Psychoanalysis,* S.E., Vol. 23, pp. 139–207.

Fromm, E., 1932a: "Psychoanalytic Characterology and Its Relevance for Social Psychology," in E. Fromm, *The Crisis of Psychoanalysis: Essays on Freud, Marx and Social Psychology* (New York: Holt, Rinehart and Winston, 1970), pp. 135–162.

————, 1936a: "Sozialpsychologischer Teil," in M. Horkheimer et al., eds., *Studien über Autorität und Familie* (Paris: Félix Alcan), pp. 77–135.

————, 1941a: *Escape from Freedom* (New York: Farrar and Rinehart).

————, 1947a: *Man for Himself: An Inquiry into the Psychology of Ethics* (New York: Rinehart).

————, 1951a: *The Forgotten Language: An Introduction to the Understanding of Dreams, Fairy Tales and Myths* (New York: Rinehart).

————, 1955a: *The Sane Society* (New York: Rinehart and Winston).

————, 1955b: "The Human Implications of Instinctivistic 'Radicalism': A Reply to Herbert Marcuse," *Dissent* (New York), pp. 342–349.

————, 1956a: *The Art of Loving* (New York: Harper and Row).

————, 1956b: "A Counter-Rebuttal to Herbert Marcuse," *Dissent* (New York), pp. 81–83.

————, 1960a: "Psychoanalysis and Zen Buddhism," in D. T. Suzuki, E. Fromm, and R. de Martino, eds., *Zen Buddhism and Psychoanalysis* (New York: Harper and Row), pp. 77–141.

————, 1964a: *The Heart of Man: Its Genius for Good and Evil* (New York: Harper and Row).

————, 1966a: *You Shall Be as Gods: A Radical Interpretation of the Old Testament and Its Tradition* (New York: Holt, Rinehart and Winston).

————, 1968h: "Marx's Contribution to the Knowledge of Man," in E. Fromm, *The Crisis of Psychoanalysis: Essays on Freud, Marx and Social Psychology* (New York: Holt, Rinehart and Winston), pp. 62–76.

————, 1970a: *The Crisis of Psychoanalysis: Essays on Freud, Marx and Social Psychology* (New York: Holt, Rinehart and Winston).

———, 1970b (together with Michael Maccoby): *Social Character in a Mexican Village: A Sociopsychoanalytic Study* (Englewood Cliffs, N.J.: Prentice-Hall).

———, 1970c: "The Crisis of Psychoanalysis," in E. Fromm, *The Crisis of Psychoanalysis: Essays on Freud, Marx and Social Psychology* (New York: Holt, Rinehart and Winston), pp. 9–41.

———, 1973a: *The Anatomy of Human Destructiveness* (New York: Holt, Rinehart and Winston).

———, 1979a: *Greatness and Limitations of Freud's Thought* (New York: Harper and Row). (English translation published in 1980.)

———, 1980a: *The Working Class in Weimar Germany: A Psychological and Sociological Study (Arbeiter und Angestellte am Vorabend des Dritten Reiches. Eine sozialpsychologische Untersuchung),* edited by Wolfgang Bonß (London: Berg Publishers).

———, 1989a: *The Art of Being* (New York, 1992: Crossroad/ Continuum). (German translation was published first under the title *Vom Haber aum Sein* in 1989.)

Gorer, G., 1934: *Marquis de Sade* (New York: Liveright Publishing Corporation).

Holt, R. R., 1965: "Freud's Cognitive Style," *American Imago,* Vol. 22, pp. 163–179.

Huxley, A., 1946: *Brave New World* (London: Vanguard Library).

Laing, R. D., 1960: *The Divided Self: An Existential Study in Sanity and Madness* (London: Tavistock Publications).

———, 1961: *The Self and Others: Further Studies in Sanity and Madness* (London: Tavistock Publications).

———, 1964a (together with D. G. Cooper): *Reason and Violence: A Decade of Sartre's Philosophy 1950–1960,* with a Foreword by Jean-Paul Sartre (London: Tavistock Publications).

———, 1964b (together with A. Esterson): *Sanity, Madness and the Family.* Volume I: *Families of Schizophrenics* (London: Tavistock Publications).

———, 1966 (together with H. Phillipson and A. R. Lee): *Interpersonal Perception: A Theory and a Method of Research* (London: Tavistock Publications).

Bibliography

————, 1967a: *The Politics of Experience* (New York: Pantheon Books).

————, 1967b: *The Politics of Experience and The Bird of Paradise* (Harmondsworth, Ind.: Penguin Books).

Maccoby, M., 1976: *The Gamesman: The New Corporate Leaders* (New York: Simon and Schuster).

Marcuse, H., 1941: *Reason and Revolution* (Cambridge, Mass.: Harvard University Press).

————, 1964: *One-Dimensional Man* (Boston: Beacon Press).

————, 1955/1966: *Eros and Civilization: A Philosophical Inquiry into Freud,* with a New Preface by the author (Boston: Beacon Press).

————, 1969: *An Essay on Liberation* (Boston: Beacon Press).

May, R., E. Angel, and H. F. Ellenberger, eds., 1958: *Existence* (New York: Basic Books).

Réage, P., 1972: *Histoire d'O* (Paris: Jean-Jacques Pauvert); in English: *The Story of O.* (New York: Grove Press, 1965).

Sartre, J.-P., 1957: *Existentialism and Human Emotions* (New York: Philosophical Library).

Sontag, S., 1969: *Styles of Radical Will* (New York: Farrar, Strauss and Giroux).

Speer, A., 1970: *Inside the Third Reich: Memoirs* (London: Weidenfeld and Nicolson).

Suzuki, D. T., 1957, personal communication.

About the Book

It was Erich Fromm's conviction that psychoanalysis needs to retain Freud's essential insight into the unconscious while replacing his mechanistic-materialistic philosophy with a humanistic one. In this book, never before published in English, Fromm presents such a revision of psychoanalysis, one that is both humanistic and dialectical.

The Revision of Psychoanalysis is Fromm's long-expected account of his own personal way of understanding and practicing psychoanalysis. Of special interest to today's readers are his continuing efforts to understand the meaning of sexuality, his critique of Herbert Marcuse's vision of psychoanalysis, and the implications of a Freudian analytical social psychology for the reform of social arrangements. This book is essential reading for psychologists and for social and political theorists in many disciplines. For psychoanalysts, it provides Fromm's most provocative and unique recommendations for the revision of psychoanalysis.

Erich Fromm (1900–1980) was not only an outstanding social scientist and author of bestsellers (*Escape from Freedom; The Art of Loving; To Have or to Be?*) but also a first-rate practicing psychoanalyst who applied his experience to the interpretation of social phenomena and reformulated Freud's basic insights into the unconscious of the individual and of society.

Rainer Funk was Erich Fromm's last assistant and is now literary executor and editor of Fromm's literary estate.

Name Index

Name Index

Kant, Immanuel, 24
Kardiner, Abraham, 65
Kierkegaard, Sören, 61
Kinsey, Alfred C., 67

Laing, Ronald D., 20, 60–63, 70, 78
Lorenz, Konrad, 6

Maccoby, Michael, 29, 66, 105
Maimonides, Moses, 43
Marcuse, Herbert, 66, 92–93, 96–97, 111–129
Marx, Karl, 12, 52, 61, 111, 114, 121–122
Masters, W. W., 67
May, Rollo, 60
Midas, 30

Narcissus, 120
Nietzsche, Friedrich, 61

Onan, 81

Paracelsus, 52
Paul VI, Pope, 82

Plato, 31

Radó, Sándor, 18
Réage, Pauline, 92
Reich, Wilhelm, 35, 66–67, 69, 87–88, 113, 123
Riesman, David, 66
Roheim, Geza, 65

Sade, Marquis de, 92
Sartre, Jean-Paul, 27, 61
Schultz, I. H., 69
Schweitzer, Albert, 52
Selver, Charlotte, 69
Shakespeare, 59
Socrates, 52
Sontag, Susan, 25
Speer, Albert, 50–51
Spinoza, Baruch de, 52, 95
Spitz, René, 47
Stalin, Joseph, 107
Sullivan, Harry Stack, 1, 17–18, 20, 61, 70
Suzuki, Daisetz T., 79

Tillich, Paul, 61

West, Ellen, 60

Subject Index